How to Make Your Money Grow

The Money Secrets Most People Never Learn

Written by A. M. Hartley

This book is published under a pseudonym.

Imprint: Independently published.

Introduction

Most of us spend a large part of our lives working to earn money.

We work hard, pay our bills, save when we can, and hope that over time our financial situation will improve. Yet many people eventually find themselves asking the same question:

"Why does it seem so much easier for some people to build wealth than others?"

The answer is often simpler than we think.
It isn't always about earning the highest income.
It isn't about being unusually lucky. And it certainly isn't because only a select few understand some hidden formula. More often, it's because many of us were never taught how money works.

We leave school knowing how to solve equations, analyse literature, or remember historical events, yet few of us are taught how to make confident financial decisions, how to recognise opportunities, or how to make our money work for us instead of always working for it.

As a result, many people learn through trial and error. Some lessons are small. Others can cost thousands of dollars and years of missed opportunities.

This book was written to help change that.

It isn't a guide to getting rich quickly, and it doesn't promise guaranteed returns. There are no shortcuts or secret formulas here. Instead, you'll discover practical, time-tested principles that have helped people build financial security over many years.

Some ideas may already be familiar. Others may be completely new. My goal is not to overwhelm you with complicated financial language, but to explain important concepts in a way that is clear, practical, and easy to understand.

If there is one message, I hope you take away before reading another page, it is this:

It is never too late to improve your financial future.

Perhaps you wish you had started saving earlier, invested sooner, or made different financial decisions in the past.

Many people feel that way.

But you cannot change yesterday's decisions. You can only decide what you will do next.

Whether you are just beginning your financial journey, rebuilding after setbacks, supporting a family, or planning for retirement, every positive decision you make today has the potential to improve your tomorrow.

Building wealth rarely happens overnight. More often, it is the result of many small, thoughtful decisions made consistently over time.

My hope is that this book gives you the knowledge and confidence to make those decisions with greater clarity.

Wherever you are starting from, you are welcome here.

Let's begin.

Chapter 1

The Biggest Money Mistakes Most People Make

Did You Know?

Many people who earn a comfortable income still struggle financially—not because they don't earn enough, but because they were never taught the habits that help money grow over time.

Building wealth isn't just about how much you earn. It's also about the decisions you make with the money you already have.

Most people don't set out to make poor financial decisions.

In fact, the vast majority of people work hard, want financial security, and genuinely try to do the right thing. They pay their bills, support their families, and save when they can. Yet despite their best efforts, many still find themselves feeling like they're running just to stand still.

Why? Often, it isn't because they lack intelligence or motivation. It's because no one ever taught them the habits and principles that allow money to grow over time.

Financial success is rarely determined by a single decision. Instead, it is usually the result of hundreds of small decisions made consistently over many years. Likewise, financial stress often develops gradually through habits that seem harmless at the time but become costly when repeated year after year.

Let's look at some of the most common mistakes.

Mistake 1: Believing a Higher Income Will Solve Everything

One of the most common beliefs is that earning more money will automatically solve financial problems.

Sometimes it does—but often it doesn't.

Many people receive pay rises throughout their careers, only to find that their savings haven't grown very much. As income increases, spending often increases as well. A larger home, a newer car, more subscriptions, more holidays, and more expensive everyday purchases slowly become the new normal.

This is often called **lifestyle inflation**.

Instead of giving yourself permission to spend every extra dollar you earn, consider directing part of every pay rise towards your future. Even saving or investing half of each increase can make a significant difference over time while still allowing you to enjoy a higher standard of living.

Mistake 2: Waiting for the "Perfect Time"

Many people delay saving or investing because they believe they'll start once life settles down. Perhaps after the next promotion. After paying off debt. After buying a home. After the children are older. The difficulty is that life rarely becomes less expensive or less busy.

Waiting for the perfect moment often means waiting forever. Starting with a small amount today is usually far more valuable than waiting years until you feel completely ready.

Mistake 3: Living Without a Plan

Imagine setting off on a long journey without knowing your destination. You might eventually arrive somewhere, but it probably won't be where you intended. Money works in much the samc way. Without clear goals, it's easy for income to disappear on everyday expenses without making meaningful progress towards financial security.

A financial plan doesn't need to be complicated. It simply needs to answer a few important questions:

- What am I working towards?
- How much will I need?
- What small steps can I take consistently?

Even simple goals can provide direction and help you make better decisions.

Mistake 4: Allowing Debt to Control Your Future

Not all debt is bad. Borrowing to purchase an asset that may grow in value or generate income can sometimes be a sensible financial decision. However, high-interest consumer debt is different. Credit cards, personal loans for unnecessary purchases, and "buy now, pay later" arrangements can quietly consume money that could otherwise have been saved or invested.

Interest works both ways. It can help grow your wealth—or it can steadily reduce it. Learning the difference is one of the most important financial lessons you'll ever learn.

Mistake 5: Thinking Small Decisions Don't Matter

Many people underestimate the power of everyday financial choices. A single purchase rarely determines your financial future. But repeated decisions do.
The coffee you buy each morning isn't the problem by itself. Neither is an occasional meal out or a weekend away.
The important question is whether your spending reflects what matters most to you. Building wealth doesn't require eliminating everything you enjoy. It requires making intentional choices and understanding that every dollar has a job. Sometimes that job is providing enjoyment today. Sometimes its job is creating freedom tomorrow. Learning to

balance both is one of the keys to long-term financial success.

The Good News

If you've recognised yourself in some of these mistakes, you're not alone. Most people have made at least one of them. Many have made several. The encouraging news is that none of these mistakes need to define your future.

Every good financial habit begins with awareness. Once you understand why money behaves the way it does, you can begin making decisions that gradually move you closer to your goals. You don't need to change everything overnight. Small improvements, repeated consistently over time, often produce remarkable results.

Key Takeaways

- Building wealth is influenced more by consistent financial habits than by income alone.
- Lifestyle inflation can quietly prevent your wealth from growing.
- Waiting for the "perfect time" often delays progress unnecessarily.
- Having a simple financial plan gives your money purpose and direction.
- Understanding the difference between good debt and bad debt is an important step towards financial security.

- Small financial decisions, repeated consistently, can have a significant impact over time.

Take a Moment

Before moving on, ask yourself:

- Which of the money mistakes in this chapter have I made?
- Which one is costing me the most?
- What is one financial habit I could improve this month?
- If I made that one change consistently for the next ten years, how different might my financial future look?

Remember, lasting financial change rarely comes from one big decision. It comes from making better decisions, one step at a time.

In the next chapter, we'll explore one of the most powerful concepts in personal finance—one that quietly rewards patience more than almost anything else. Compound interest.

THE WEALTH JOURNEY

Small steps today. A better future tomorrow.

Building wealth isn't about getting rich quickly.
It's about following a simple path, staying consistent, and letting time do the hard work.

1 EARN
Create income through your job, skills, or business. Your income is the starting point of your journey.

→

2 SAVE
Spend less than you earn.
Saving gives you control and creates financial breathing room.

↓

3 BUILD AN EMERGENCY FUND
Set aside 3–6 months of living expenses.
This protects you when life throws you a curveball.

→

4 INVEST
Put your money to work so it can grow over time.
Start early and be consistent, even if it's small.

↓

5 GROW WEALTH
Let compounding and time do the heavy lifting.
Your money grows, even while you sleep.

→

6 PROTECT WEALTH
Protect what you've built with insurance, an emergency fund, and smart decisions.

↓

7 CREATE PASSIVE INCOME
Build income streams that earn for you.
This gives you more freedom and choices.

→

8 FINANCIAL FREEDOM
Live life on your terms. Work because you choose to, not because you have to.

This isn't a get-rich-quick plan.
It's a proven path to lasting wealth and a more secure future.

Be patient. Stay consistent. Keep learning. The journey to wealth is a marathon, not a sprint.

Chapter 2

The Power of Compound Interest

Did You Know?

Two people can invest the same amount of money and achieve very different outcomes simply because one started earlier.

When it comes to building wealth, time is often one of your greatest advantages.

Imagine planting a single tree.

In its first year, it grows a little. The next year it grows a little more. Before long, it becomes large enough to produce seeds of its own. Those seeds grow into new trees, which eventually produce even more seeds. Over time, what began as a single tree can become an entire forest.

Money can grow in a remarkably similar way.

When your savings or investments earn interest or generate returns, those earnings can begin earning returns of their own. Instead of growth occurring only on the money you originally invested, growth starts occurring on previous growth as well.

This is known as **compound interest**, and it is one of the most powerful forces in long-term wealth building.

At first, the progress often feels slow.

In fact, many people become discouraged during the early years because they don't see dramatic results. But compound growth isn't designed to impress you in the beginning. Its real strength becomes visible over time.

This is why patience matters so much.

The Snowball Effect

Picture yourself standing at the top of a snowy hill. You roll a small snowball down the slope. At first, it barely changes. Then, as it continues rolling, it gathers more snow. It becomes larger, heavier, and begins collecting even more snow than before. The bigger it becomes, the faster it grows.
Compound interest works much the same way.

Your money begins by growing slowly. As your balance increases, each year's growth has a larger amount to work with, allowing future growth to become even greater. The hardest part is often staying patient long enough to see the snowball gather momentum.

Example

Sophie invests $200 each month from age 25.

Daniel waits until age 35 before investing the same amount each month.

Both invest consistently, but Sophie gives her money an extra ten years to grow through compound interest. Over time, those additional years can make a remarkable difference to the final value of her investments.

Time Is Your Greatest Advantage

Many people believe they need thousands of dollars before investing. In reality, time is often far more valuable than the amount you start with. Someone who invests modest amounts consistently over many years may finish with considerably more wealth than someone who waits until they can afford larger investments.

The earlier you begin, the more opportunity your money has to grow. That doesn't mean you've missed your chance if you're starting later. Far from it. Every year your money is invested gives it another opportunity to grow. The important thing is to begin.

It's Never Too Late

One of the biggest reasons people never start investing is because they believe they've already left it too late.

Perhaps you're thinking: *"If only I'd started ten years ago."* You're probably right. Starting earlier would likely have produced a better outcome. But there is another way to look at it. Ten years from now, you'll either be grateful you started today, or you'll wish you had.

The past cannot be changed.

The future can. Whether you're in your twenties, forties, sixties, or beyond, making better financial decisions today is almost always better than waiting for tomorrow.

Consistency Beats Perfection

Many people spend months researching investments because they're afraid of making the wrong decision. While learning is important, waiting forever has its own cost. In many cases, investing a sensible amount regularly over many years is more valuable than trying to perfectly time every market movement.
You don't have to invest perfectly. You simply need to invest consistently. Small amounts invested month after month can become surprisingly significant over decades.

Patience Is Part of the Strategy

Modern life encourages immediate results. We expect fast internet, instant purchases, same-day delivery, and quick answers. Building wealth works differently. There will be periods when your investments appear to make little progress. There will be years when markets rise and years when they fall. This is normal. Successful investors understand that short-term fluctuations are part of a much longer journey.

Rather than focusing on what happened this week or this month, they continue following their plan.

Over time, patience often becomes one of the greatest contributors to financial success.

Key Takeaways

- Compound interest allows your money to earn returns on both your original investment and the returns it has already earned.
- Time is often more valuable than investing a large amount at the beginning.
- Starting today is usually better than waiting for the perfect moment.
- Consistency is often more important than trying to invest perfectly.
- Patience gives compound interest the time it needs to produce meaningful results.

Take a Moment

Before you move on, pause for a moment and ask yourself:

- If I started investing today, where could I be in 10 or 20 years?
- What has stopped me from starting until now?

- What is one small financial decision I could make this week that my future self would thank me for?

Remember, building wealth doesn't begin with a large investment.

It begins with a decision.

The most powerful investment advantage isn't finding the perfect share or predicting the next market trend. It’s giving your money enough time to grow.

In the next chapter, we'll look at something much simpler—but often overlooked—how to make your savings work harder, even before you begin investing.

COMPOUND INTEREST

The Eighth Wonder of the World

Compound interest means you earn interest on your money, and then earn interest on that interest.

HOW IT WORKS

The earlier you start, the more time your money has to grow.

Small amounts over time can grow into something big.

KEY IDEA

Time is more important than timing.

THE POWER OF TIME

If you invest $200 per month at an average return of 7% per year, here's how it could grow:

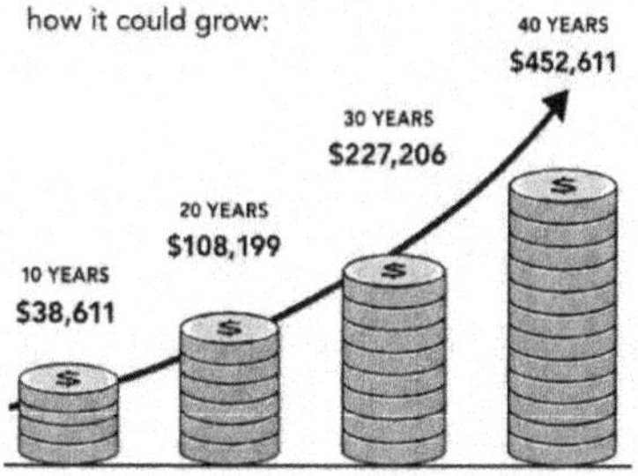

The amount you invest stays the same.
The time makes the difference.

EXAMPLE

- You invest $200 per month
- Average return 7% per year
- Start early and stay consistent
- Reinvest your returns and watch it grow

TWO PEOPLE. SAME INVESTMENT.

STARTS AT AGE 25 Invests $200 per month Stops at age 35 → Invested for 10 years	**STARTS AT AGE 35** Invests $200 per month Continues until age 65 → Invested for 30 years
VALUE AT AGE 65 **$1,043,142**	VALUE AT AGE 65 **$1,042,306**

VS.

REMEMBER

Start early.
Be consistent.
Let time do
the heavy lifting.

COMPOUND INTEREST REWARDS PATIENCE AND CONSISTENCY.
The best time to start was yesterday.
The second best time is today.

Small steps today.
Big results tomorrow.

Chapter 3

Make Saving Work Harder

Did You Know?

Leaving money in an account that earns little or no interest means inflation can gradually reduce what that money is able to buy.

Making your savings work harder doesn't always require taking more risk. Sometimes it simply means choosing a better place to keep your money.

Saving money is one of the first financial habits most of us learn.

As children, we might have been given a piggy bank or encouraged to put birthday money aside for something special. As adults, saving often becomes about something much bigger—creating security, preparing for unexpected expenses, and building the foundation for future wealth.

Yet many people make one simple mistake. They save their money, but they don't make it work. Money sitting in a bank account that pays little or no interest is safe, but it isn't working very hard for you. While your balance may stay the same, inflation quietly reduces what that money can buy over time.

Imagine leaving $10,000 untouched for many years. If prices continue to rise while your savings earn very little interest, that $10,000 will buy less in the future than it can today. That's why it's important to think beyond simply saving money. The goal is to save wisely.

Understanding High-Interest Savings Accounts

For many people, a high-interest savings account is one of the easiest ways to make their money work a little harder while still keeping it readily available.

These accounts generally pay a higher rate of interest than everyday transaction accounts, allowing your savings to grow without requiring you to invest in the share market or other assets.

Some high-interest accounts require you to meet certain conditions, such as depositing a minimum amount each month or making only limited withdrawals. Others may offer an introductory interest rate that changes after a period of time.

For this reason, it's worth comparing different accounts and understanding the conditions before opening one. A small difference in interest rates may not seem significant at first, but over many years it can make a noticeable difference.

Example

Emma keeps $10,000 in a transaction account that earns almost no interest.

Jake keeps the same $10,000 in a high-interest savings account.

Both still have access to their money, but Jake earns interest while he saves.

Build an Emergency Fund First

Before investing, it's usually wise to have money set aside for unexpected events. Cars break down. Hot water systems fail. Medical expenses arise. Employment circumstances can change. Without savings, these situations often lead to borrowing money, sometimes at high interest rates.

An emergency fund provides breathing room. It allows you to deal with life's unexpected moments without immediately reaching for a credit card or personal loan. There is no single amount that suits everyone. The right emergency fund depends on your personal circumstances, income, family responsibilities, and financial commitments. The important thing is simply to begin building one. Even a modest emergency fund can reduce financial stress and provide greater confidence.

Saving Has a Purpose

Saving isn't just about accumulating money. Every dollar you save should have a purpose.

Perhaps you're saving for:

- A home deposit.
- Travel.
- Education.
- A business opportunity.
- Retirement.
- Financial independence.
- Peace of mind.

Having a clear purpose makes saving easier because each dollar feels like progress rather than sacrifice. When you know why you're saving, you're often less tempted to spend impulsively.

Saving Is the Foundation of Investing

Some people believe saving and investing are completely separate. In reality, they work together. Saving creates the opportunity to invest. Without savings, there is little money available to purchase assets that may grow over time. Think of saving as building the foundation of a house. Investing is what you build on top of it. A strong foundation provides stability for everything that follows.

Don't Chase Every Opportunity

As your confidence grows, you'll probably encounter advertisements promising extraordinary investment returns. Be cautious, if something sounds too good to be true, it often is. Building wealth usually isn't exciting.

It is more often the result of making sensible decisions consistently over many years. There will always be another investment opportunity. There will never be another opportunity to undo a reckless financial decision.

Patience and discipline are often far more valuable than chasing quick profits.

Key Takeaways

- Saving money is important but making your savings work harder is even better.
- High-interest savings accounts can help your money grow while remaining accessible.
- An emergency fund provides financial security and helps reduce the need for high-interest debt.
- Giving your savings a clear purpose makes it easier to stay motivated.
- Saving and investing work together, with saving providing the foundation for future wealth.
- Building wealth usually rewards patience and consistency rather than chasing quick returns.

Take a Moment

Before moving on, ask yourself:

- Is my savings account working as hard as it could be?
- Do I have an emergency fund, or is that something I need to build?
- What am I saving for?
- Is there one simple change I could make this month to help my savings grow?

Remember, every investment journey begins with money that was first saved.

In the next chapter, we'll look at debt. Not all debt is harmful, and understanding the difference between good debt and bad debt could save you thousands of dollars over your lifetime.

EMERGENCY FUND
(Three Jars)

A simple system to help you manage your money with confidence, handle surprises, and build your future.

1 EVERYDAY SPENDING
Your day-to-day money.
For regular expenses.

2 EMERGENCY FUND
Your safety net.
For life's unexpected moments.

3 INVESTMENTS
Your future builder.
For long-term growth.

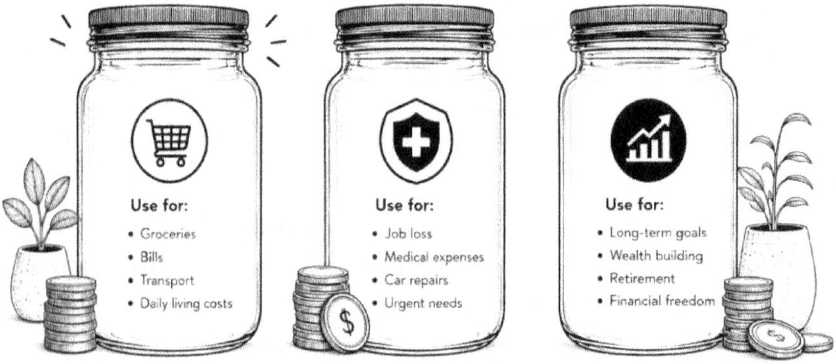

Keep this money accessible for your everyday needs.

Aim for 3–6 months of essential expenses.
Keep it separate. Don't touch it unless it's a real emergency.

Invest for the future, not for emergencies.
Let your money grow.

HOW IT WORKS

1. Fund Jar 1 first – cover your monthly living expenses.
2. Build Jar 2 – create your emergency fund.
3. Grow Jar 3 – invest consistently for your future.

KEY REMINDERS

✓ Keep your emergency fund in a separate, easy-to-access account.
✓ Only use it for real emergencies.
✓ Review your jars regularly and adjust as your life changes.

Plan today.
Protect today.
Build your tomorrow.
♥

Chapter 4

Good Debt vs Bad Debt

> **Did You Know?**
>
> Interest can work in two very different ways. It can help grow your wealth when you invest, or it can quietly reduce your wealth when you're paying it to someone else. Understanding the difference is one of the most important financial lessons you can learn.

Debt often has a bad reputation. Many people grow up believing that all debt should be avoided at all costs. While reducing unnecessary debt is certainly a worthwhile goal, the reality is a little more complex. Not all debt is the same.

Some forms of borrowing can help build wealth over time, while others can quietly make it much harder to achieve financial security. The key is understanding the difference.

What Is Bad Debt?

Bad debt is money borrowed to purchase something that loses value or provides only short-term enjoyment while the repayments continue long after the benefit has disappeared.

Common examples include:

- Credit card debt that isn't paid off each month.
- Personal loans for holidays.
- Borrowing to buy luxury items you cannot comfortably afford.
- "Buy now, pay later" purchases that accumulate over time.

These types of debt often carry high interest rates. The longer they remain unpaid, the more expensive they become. In many cases, you end up paying far more than the original purchase price. A small purchase today can quietly become a much larger expense over the following months or years.

What Is Good Debt?

Good debt is borrowing that has the potential to improve your financial position over time. This doesn't mean it is risk-free. Rather, it means the money has been borrowed to purchase something that may increase in value or generate income.
Examples may include:

- Purchasing a home.
- Buying an investment property.
- Borrowing to invest in a business.
- Education or training that significantly improves future earning potential.

Even with these examples, borrowing should always be approached carefully. Good debt can become bad debt if repayments become unaffordable or unnecessary risks are taken.

Example

Sarah borrows $25,000 to buy a reliable car she needs for work.

Ben borrows $25,000 on a credit card for holidays and expensive gadgets.

Both borrowed the same amount, but one loan helped create opportunities while the other financed short-term spending.

The Cost of Interest

Whenever you borrow money, you're paying for the privilege of using someone else's money. That payment is called interest. The higher the interest rate, the more expensive borrowing becomes.
Many people focus only on the size of their monthly repayments. A more important question is: **"How much will this cost me in total?"** Looking at the total amount repaid over the life of a loan often tells a very different story. Understanding the true cost of borrowing helps you make better financial decisions.

Borrow With Purpose

Before taking on any debt, it can be helpful to pause and ask yourself a few simple questions.

- Do I truly need this?
- Could I save for it instead?
- Will this purchase improve my financial future?

- Can I comfortably afford the repayments if my circumstances change?
- Am I borrowing because I want it now rather than because I genuinely need it?

These questions won't eliminate every poor financial decision, but they can prevent many of them.
Sometimes waiting a little longer is the smartest financial choice you can make.

Debt Should Never Control Your Life

Debt becomes dangerous when it removes your freedom. If repayments prevent you from saving, investing, or coping with unexpected expenses, your financial future becomes increasingly fragile.
The goal isn't necessarily to avoid all debt.
The goal is to make sure your debt is working for you rather than against you. When debt helps build assets or improve future opportunities, it may have a place in a long-term financial plan. When debt simply funds today's lifestyle at tomorrow's expense, it often becomes an obstacle to wealth.

Financial Freedom Starts With Better Decisions

Many people think financial freedom comes from earning more money. Sometimes it does.
But just as often, it comes from reducing unnecessary financial commitments. Every loan you repay.
Every credit card balance you eliminate. Every unnecessary interest payment you avoid. Each one

leaves more of your income available to save, invest, and build your future. Over time, these decisions create momentum, and momentum is a powerful thing.

Key Takeaways

- Not all debt is the same; understanding the difference is essential.
- Bad debt often finances short-term wants while creating long-term financial costs.
- Good debt has the potential to build wealth or increase future earning capacity.
- Always consider the total cost of borrowing, not just the monthly repayment.
- Borrow with purpose and only when it supports your long-term financial goals.
- Reducing unnecessary debt creates more opportunities to save and invest.

Take a Moment

Before moving on, ask yourself:

- Do I currently have debt that is helping me or holding me back?
- Are there repayments I could reduce or eliminate over time?
- Before my next major purchase, will I stop and ask whether I truly need it?

- What would my financial future look like if more of my income stayed in my own pocket?

Remember, every dollar you don't pay in unnecessary interest is a dollar that can help build your future.

In the next chapter, we'll begin exploring how to put your money to work through investing, and why you don't need to be wealthy before you can get started.

GOOD DEBT vs BAD DEBT

Not all debt is the same.

Good debt can help you build a better future.
Bad debt can hold you back.

GOOD DEBT

Invests in your future and can help build wealth.

VS

BAD DEBT

Used for short-term wants and can keep you stuck.

GOOD DEBT	BAD DEBT
EDUCATION LOANS Helps you gain skills and knowledge that can lead to higher income.	**CREDIT CARD DEBT** High interest rates for everyday spending can quickly spiral out of control.
HOME LOAN Buying a home can provide security and may grow in value over time.	**SHOPPING SPREES** Borrowing for things you want, not things you need.
BUSINESS LOANS Used to start or grow a business that can generate income.	**HOLIDAYS AND LUXURIES** Financing holidays or luxury items doesn't build your future.
INVESTMENT LOANS Borrowing to invest (carefully and wisely) can grow wealth over time.	**PAYDAY LOANS** Very high interest rates and fees make it hard to ever get ahead.
Typical Interest Rates: Lower (e.g. home loan 5–6% p.a.*)	**Typical Interest Rates: Higher** (e.g. credit card 15–20%+ p.a.*)

*Rates are examples only and can change.

Use debt as a tool, not a trap.
When used wisely, debt can open doors.
When used carelessly, it can lock you in.

Chapter 5

Investing Without Being Rich

> **Did You Know?**
>
> One of the biggest reasons people never start investing is because they believe they don't have enough money. In reality, many successful investors began with small amounts and simply remained consistent over time.

For many people, investing feels like something reserved for the wealthy. It's easy to picture successful investors as people with large salaries, expensive suits, and hundreds of thousands of dollars ready to invest.

The reality is often very different. Many people begin with modest amounts. What separates successful investors from everyone else is rarely how much they start with. It's that they start.

You Don't Need Thousands of Dollars

Years ago, investing often required larger amounts of money. Today, that's no longer the case.

Many investment platforms allow people to begin investing with relatively small amounts. The exact amount isn't what matters most. Developing the habit of investing regularly is.

Small, consistent investments made over many years often produce far better results than waiting until you have what feels like "enough." Remember, your first investment isn't about becoming wealthy overnight. It's about building a habit that can last for decades.

Example

Chloe starts investing $50 each week.

It doesn't feel like much.

After one year she has invested over $2,600 before any investment growth.

Don't Wait Until You Know Everything

One mistake many people make is believing they need to become an expert before investing. Learning is important. Understanding risk is important. Knowing what you're investing in is important. But waiting until you know absolutely everything can become another reason never to begin.

Even experienced investors continue learning throughout their lives. You don't need perfect knowledge. You simply need enough understanding to make thoughtful, informed decisions. Knowledge grows with experience.

Consistency Beats Timing

You've probably heard people ask questions like: "Is now the right time to invest?" While market conditions certainly matter, many people spend years waiting for the perfect opportunity. Unfortunately, nobody consistently predicts exactly when markets will rise or fall.

Rather than trying to perfectly time every investment, many successful investors focus on investing regularly.
Sometimes prices are higher, sometimes they're lower.
Over time, regular investing allows you to buy across different market conditions instead of relying on one perfect moment. This approach also removes much of the emotion from investing. Instead of worrying about headlines every day, you simply continue following your plan.

Investing Is a Marathon

Modern media often celebrates people who become wealthy very quickly. Those stories attract attention because they're unusual. Most long-term wealth is built much more quietly. It grows through patience. Regular investing. Allowing time to do the heavy lifting.

The investors who quietly continue through good years and difficult years often achieve better results than those constantly chasing the next exciting opportunity.

Every Dollar Has a Job

Whenever you receive income, every dollar has a purpose. Some pays your living expenses; some provides enjoyment today. Some should be working for your future. The earlier you begin giving part of your income that job, the longer it has to work on your behalf.

Over many years, those dollars can begin producing more dollars. That's when investing becomes truly powerful.

Building Confidence

It's perfectly normal to feel nervous before making your first investment. Almost everyone does. Confidence doesn't usually come before taking action.

It grows because you've taken action. You don't have to invest everything at once. You don't need to chase the highest returns. You simply need to begin thoughtfully and continue learning along the way.

Key Takeaways

- You don't need to be wealthy before you can begin investing.
- Building the habit of investing regularly is often more important than the amount you start with.
- Waiting until you know everything may prevent you from ever getting started.

- Consistency usually beats trying to perfectly time the market.
- Long-term investing rewards patience more than excitement.
- Confidence grows through experience, not perfection.

Take a Moment

Before moving on, ask yourself:

- Have I been waiting until I have "enough" money before investing?
- What's really stopping me from getting started?
- Could I comfortably invest a small amount each month?
- How might those small investments grow over the next 10, 20, or 30 years?

Remember, the size of your first investment matters far less than making your first investment.

In the next chapter, we'll explore shares and dividends, and how owning part of a company can allow your money to grow in more than one way.

Chapter 6

Shares and Dividends

> **Did You Know?**
>
> When you buy shares in a company, you're not simply buying a number on a screen. You're buying a small ownership stake in a real business that employs people, sells products or services, and hopes to grow over time.
>
> As that business grows, your investment may grow with it.

For many people, the share market feels confusing. There are charts, numbers, financial news, unfamiliar terms, and constant headlines about markets rising or falling. It's easy to feel that investing in shares is something only experts understand. Fortunately, it doesn't have to be that complicated. At its simplest, buying a share means buying a small piece of a company.

What Is a Share?

Imagine your favourite company. Perhaps it's a business whose products you use regularly or one you've watched grow over many years. Large companies are often divided into millions, sometimes billions, of small ownership pieces called shares.

When you purchase one of those shares, you become a part-owner of that business. Although your ownership may be very small, you still share in the company's success—and, like any investment, you also share in its risks.

How Shares Can Make Money

Shares generally have two ways of creating wealth.

The first is **capital growth**.

If the company becomes more valuable over time, the price of its shares may increase. If you later sell those shares for more than you paid, you've made a capital gain.

The second is **dividends**.

Some companies choose to share part of their profits with shareholders by making dividend payments.

These payments may be made regularly, depending on the company and its financial performance.

Not every company pays dividends. Some prefer to reinvest their profits back into growing the business. Others pay dividends because they generate consistent profits and want to reward their shareholders. Neither approach is automatically better. It depends on the company's goals and your investment objectives.

Example

You own 100 shares in a company.

The company pays a dividend of $2 per share.

You receive $200.

You can spend it or reinvest it to buy more shares.

The Power of Reinvesting Dividends

Many investors choose not to spend the dividends they receive. Instead, they reinvest them. This means using those dividend payments to buy additional shares. Those additional shares may then earn dividends of their own. Over time, this creates another form of compound growth.

Your investment isn't just growing because the share price may increase. It's also growing because your dividends are helping you own even more of the company. This is one reason long-term investors often place significant value on reinvesting dividends whenever possible.

Share Prices Go Up and Down

One of the most important things to understand is that share prices don't move in a straight line. Some days they rise. Other days they fall. Sometimes markets remain uncertain for weeks, months, or even longer.
This is completely normal.

Short-term price movements don't necessarily reflect the long-term quality of a business. Successful investors understand that temporary declines are part of investing. Rather than reacting emotionally to every headline, they focus on the bigger picture.

Think Like an Owner

Instead of asking, *“What will this share do tomorrow?”*

Consider asking, *“Would I be happy owning part of this business for many years?”* This simple shift in thinking encourages a long-term perspective. It reminds you that investing isn't about guessing tomorrow's price. It’s about owning quality businesses that have the potential to grow over time.

Diversification Matters

Even excellent companies can experience difficult periods. That's why many investors avoid putting all of their money into a single company. Owning investments across different businesses and industries helps reduce risk.

This approach is known as **diversification**.

In the next chapter, you'll discover one of the simplest ways many people achieve diversification without needing to choose dozens of individual companies themselves.

Key Takeaways

- Buying shares means becoming a part-owner of a business.
- Shares can generate wealth through capital growth and dividends.
- Reinvesting dividends can further accelerate long-term growth.
- Share prices naturally rise and fall over time.
- Long-term investors focus on the quality of the business rather than short-term price movements.
- Diversification helps reduce investment risk.

Take a Moment

Before moving on, ask yourself:

- Have I thought of shares as ownership in a business, or simply as numbers on a screen?
- Would I be comfortable owning part of a company for many years?
- How would I feel if the value of my investment temporarily fell?
- Am I prepared to think long term rather than react to short-term market movements?

Remember, successful investing is often less about predicting the future and more about remaining patient while good businesses continue to grow.

In the next chapter, we'll explore Exchange Traded Funds (ETFs) and why many experienced investors believe they are one of the simplest ways to build a diversified investment portfolio.

Chapter 7

ETFs: Investing the Simple Way

> **Did You Know?**
>
> Many professional investors don't try to pick the next winning company. Instead, they invest in funds that own hundreds—or even thousands—of companies at the same time. This approach helps spread risk and makes investing much simpler.

By now, you've learned what it means to own shares in a company. You may also be wondering: *"How do I choose which companies to invest in?"* It's a good question.

The truth is, choosing individual companies takes time, research, and ongoing attention. Even experienced investors don't always get it right. Fortunately, there is another approach that many people find simpler.

It's called an **Exchange Traded Fund**, or **ETF**.

What Is an ETF?

An ETF is an investment fund that holds a collection of investments instead of just one.

Rather than buying shares in a single company, buying an ETF often means you're buying small ownership interests in many companies at once. Some ETFs hold hundreds of companies. Others hold thousands. The exact investments depend on the purpose of the ETF. Some focus on large companies. Some focus on particular industries. Others track entire share markets.

Example

Instead of buying shares in one company, you buy one ETF that holds shares in 200 different companies.

If one company performs poorly, the other 199 help reduce the overall impact on your investment.

Why Many People Choose ETFs

Imagine trying to build a football team. Would you rather rely on one player or have an entire team working together? Investing can be similar. If you own shares in only one company, your investment depends heavily on how that single business performs.

If you own hundreds of companies through an ETF, one company's poor performance is less likely to have a major impact on your overall investment. This is one of the biggest advantages of diversification. Rather than placing all your eggs in one basket, you're spreading your investment across many businesses.

ETFs Don't Eliminate Risk

It's important to understand that no investment is completely risk-free. The value of an ETF can still rise and fall. If the overall market declines, the value of many ETFs may decline as well. However, because an ETF holds many different investments, the risk associated with one individual company is reduced. This doesn't remove risk. It helps spread it.

Keep It Simple

One mistake some investors make is believing they need dozens of different investments. Sometimes, simplicity is more effective. Many long-term investors build successful portfolios using only a small number of carefully chosen investments.

The goal isn't to own everything. The goal is to own investments that match your long-term plan. Keeping your investment strategy simple also makes it easier to remain consistent during periods of market uncertainty.

Fees Matter

Whenever you invest, it's worth understanding what fees you're paying. Even small annual fees can reduce your investment returns over many years. This doesn't mean choosing the cheapest investment available. It simply means understanding what you're paying and ensuring you receive value in return. Over decades, keeping unnecessary costs low can make a meaningful difference.

Stay Focused on the Long Term

Markets will always experience ups and downs. There will be positive headlines. There will be negative headlines. Some years your investments may perform exceptionally well. Other years may be disappointing.

These fluctuations are a normal part of investing. Rather than reacting to every change, successful investors usually focus on their long-term plan. They understand that wealth is often built through consistency, patience, and allowing time to work in their favour.

Key Takeaways

- ETFs allow you to invest in many companies through a single investment.
- Diversification helps reduce the risk associated with individual companies.
- ETFs simplify investing for many people.
- No investment is completely risk-free, including ETFs.
- Understanding investment fees is an important part of long-term wealth building.
- Staying focused on your long-term plan is often more important than reacting to short-term market movements.

Take a Moment

Before moving on, ask yourself:

- Does the idea of owning many companies appeal to me more than choosing individual shares?
- Would a simple investment strategy suit my personality better?
- Am I likely to stay invested during market ups and downs?
- How important is simplicity when building my financial future?

Remember, investing doesn't need to be complicated to be effective. Often, the simplest strategies are the ones people successfully follow for decades.

In the next chapter, we'll explore property and home ownership, including why buying a home is not always the same as making an investment, and how different property strategies may fit into a long-term wealth-building plan.

DIVERSIFICATION

Don't put all your eggs in one basket.

Diversification means spreading your investments across different assets so that your money is not dependent on a single investment doing well.

NOT DIVERSIFIED

All your money in one investment

VS

DIVERSIFIED

Your money spread across many investments

If this investment goes down, you could **lose everything.**

HIGH RISK

One poor result can have a big impact on your overall wealth.

If one investment goes down, the others may **help balance the impact.**

LOWER RISK

Different investments perform differently at different times, helping protect your wealth.

EXAMPLES OF ASSETS YOU CAN DIVERSIFY ACROSS

PROPERTY
Long-term growth and rental income

SHARES
Ownership in companies

BONDS
Regular interest income

ETFs / INDEX FUNDS
Instant diversification across many assets

CASH / TERM DEPOSITS
Lower risk and capital stability

ALTERNATIVE INVESTMENTS
e.g. commodities, infrastructure, private equity, etc.

Diversification doesn't guarantee profits or protect against loss, but it can reduce risk and give your money the best chance to grow over the long term.

Spread your investments. Protect your future.

Chapter 8

Property and Home Ownership

> **Did You Know?**
>
> For many people, buying a home will be the largest financial decision they ever make. But owning a home and building wealth are not always the same thing. Understanding the difference can help you make more informed financial decisions.

Property has long been seen as one of the most reliable ways to build wealth. For many people, owning a home represents security, stability, and a place to create memories. For others, property can also become an investment that generates income and grows in value over time.

While property can play an important role in building wealth, it is important to understand that not every property purchase is automatically a good investment. Like any financial decision, buying property should be guided by careful planning rather than emotion.

Buying a Home

For many people, purchasing their first home is an exciting milestone. It provides a place to call your own and can offer a sense of stability that renting may not provide. Over time, as you repay your mortgage, you gradually build equity. Equity is simply the difference between what your property is worth and how much you still owe on your home loan.

An Example of Equity

Imagine you buy a home for **$600,000**.

You make a **$100,000** deposit and borrow **$500,000** from the bank.

Several years later, you have reduced your home loan to **$430,000**.

During that time, the value of your home has increased to **$700,000**.

Your equity is the difference between your home's value and the amount you still owe.

Home value: $700,000

Amount still owing on your loan: $430,000

Your equity: $270,000

This means you own $270,000 of your home outright.

Equity can grow in two ways: by paying down your home loan and, if your property's value increases over time, by the home becoming more valuable.

Many homeowners build significant wealth simply by steadily reducing their mortgage over many years while benefiting from any long-term growth in their property's value.

A Home Is More Than an Investment

While people often talk about homes as investments, it's important to remember that a family home is also a place to live.

Its value cannot always be measured in dollars. A home provides shelter, security, and stability. For many families, those benefits are just as important as any financial return. Buying a home should therefore be a decision that considers both your lifestyle and your long-term financial goals.

Investment Property

Some people choose to purchase property as an investment rather than as a place to live. An investment property may generate rental income while also increasing in value over time. Like any investment, however, there are no guarantees. Property values can rise. They can also fall. Unexpected maintenance costs, vacancies, higher interest rates, and changes in the economy can all affect the return you receive. Property investing should therefore be approached with careful research and realistic expectations.

Borrow Within Your Means

One of the biggest mistakes people make is borrowing the maximum amount a lender is prepared to offer. Just because a bank is willing to lend you a certain amount doesn't necessarily mean it's the right amount for your circumstances. Life changes, interest rates can rise. Unexpected expenses happen.

Leaving yourself some financial breathing room can reduce stress and make it easier to continue saving and investing while paying your mortgage. Sometimes buying a slightly less expensive property today creates greater financial freedom tomorrow.

Imagine This...

Daniel and Sarah both purchase their first home.

Daniel chooses the largest loan the bank is willing to approve. His repayments leave very little room for savings, and unexpected expenses quickly become stressful.

Sarah buys a more modest home. Her repayments are manageable, allowing her to continue saving and investing each month.

Ten years later, both own homes. But Sarah has also built an investment portfolio because she gave herself room to keep building wealth instead of stretching every dollar.

Sometimes buying less today creates more opportunities tomorrow.

Country Differences Matter

The basic principles of property ownership are similar around the world, but the financial products available can differ from one country to another.

For example, in Australia, many home loans offer **offset accounts**. An offset account is a transaction or savings account linked to your mortgage. The money held in the account reduces the balance on which your home loan interest is calculated.

This can reduce the amount of interest you pay over the life of your loan while still allowing you access to your savings if you need them.

Other countries may offer different products that provide similar benefits, so it's worth understanding the options available where you live.

Property Is One Part of a Wealth Plan

It's easy to become focused on property alone.

However, building wealth doesn't require putting all your money into a single asset.

Many financially successful people own property while also investing in shares, ETFs, retirement accounts, businesses, or other assets.

Diversification helps reduce risk and provides more than one opportunity for your wealth to grow.

Property can be an excellent foundation, but it doesn't need to be your only strategy.

Key Takeaways

- Buying a home and building wealth are related, but they are not exactly the same.
- A family home provides both financial and lifestyle benefits.
- Investment properties can generate income and long-term growth, but they also involve risks.
- Borrowing less than your maximum borrowing capacity can provide greater financial flexibility.
- Financial products differ between countries, so understand the options available where you live.
- Property can be an important part of a diversified wealth-building strategy.

Take a Moment

Before moving on, ask yourself:

- If I already own a home, is my mortgage structured in the most effective way?

- If I hope to buy a home one day, what steps could I begin taking now?
- Would I rather own one expensive property or have room to build other investments as well?
- Am I making housing decisions based on long-term financial goals or short-term emotions?

Remember, your home is one of the biggest financial decisions you are ever likely to make.

Taking the time to make thoughtful decisions today may benefit you for many years to come.

In the next chapter, we'll explore retirement investing and why giving your money decades to grow can make an extraordinary difference to your future.

UNDERSTANDING EQUITY

Equity is the difference between what your property is worth and what you still owe on your home loan.

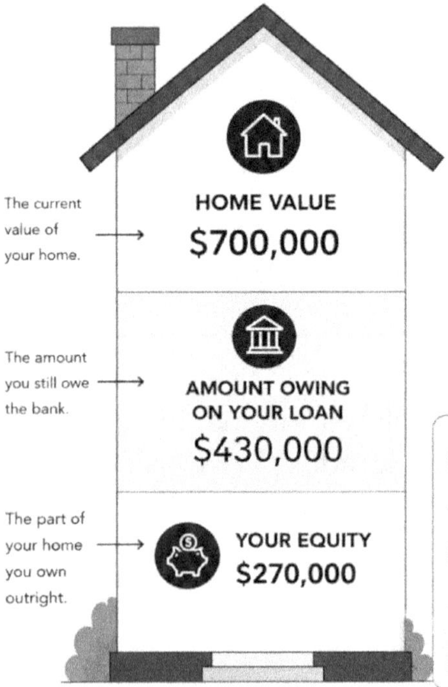

AN EXAMPLE

Imagine you bought a home for $600,000.

You made a $100,000 deposit and borrowed $500,000.

Several years later, the value of your home has increased and you have paid down some of your loan.

Here's how your equity is calculated:

Current home value	**$700,000**
Amount still owing on your loan	**– $430,000**
YOUR EQUITY	**$270,000**

EQUITY CAN GROW IN TWO WAYS:

1. By paying down your home loan.

2. If your property's value increases over time.

Over time, equity can be a powerful way to build wealth.

Your home is more than a place to live—it can be one of your greatest financial assets.

Chapter 9

Retirement Investing

Did You Know?

Many people underestimate how much time they will spend in retirement. If you retire at 65 and live until 90, your savings may need to support you for 25 years or more. The earlier you begin preparing, the more choices you may have later in life.

Retirement can seem a long way off. If you're young, it may feel like something you'll think about "one day." If you're closer to retirement, you may wonder whether you've left it too late to make a meaningful difference. The truth is that retirement planning isn't really about age. It's about giving yourself choices.

Financial security in retirement can provide the freedom to spend more time with family, travel, pursue hobbies, volunteer, or simply enjoy life without the same financial pressures that often come with full-time work. The earlier you begin preparing, the more time your money has to grow. But even if you're starting later than you hoped, every positive financial decision still has value.

Example

Increasing your retirement savings by just $20 a week may not seem like much today.

Over many years, those additional contributions—and the investment growth they generate—can add up to a substantial difference in retirement savings.

Retirement Is About More Than Stopping Work

Many people think retirement simply means finishing work. For others, it means having the freedom to choose. Some people continue working because they enjoy it, others reduce their hours or begin a new career that brings them greater satisfaction.

Financial preparation gives you options. The goal isn't necessarily to stop working. The goal is to ensure that work remains a choice rather than a necessity.

Start Earlier If You Can

Throughout this book, we've seen how powerful time can be.

Retirement investing is another example.

Money invested over several decades has more opportunity to benefit from compound growth. This doesn't mean you should feel discouraged if you're beginning later. It simply means you may need a different strategy. Starting today will almost always produce a better outcome than waiting another five or ten years.

Use the Opportunities Available to You

Many countries encourage retirement saving through specialised retirement accounts. These accounts often provide tax advantages or other incentives designed to help people prepare for the future. For example, in Australia, compulsory employer contributions are generally paid into **superannuation**, commonly known as **super**.

In other countries, different retirement savings accounts may exist. Understanding the options available where you live can make a meaningful difference over the long term. If you're unsure how your country's retirement system works, taking the time to learn about it may be one of the most valuable financial investments you ever make.

Imagine This...

Maria and Chris are both 45 years old.

Maria decides retirement is still many years away and tells herself she'll start taking it seriously later.

Chris spends an afternoon reviewing his retirement savings. He increases his regular contributions by a small amount each pay and takes the time to understand the investment options available to him.

Neither of them becomes wealthy overnight.

But twenty years later, Chris has given his money twenty more years to grow.

Small decisions made consistently often become significant over time.

Review Your Progress

Retirement planning isn't something you do once and forget. Life changes, income changes and goals change. It's worth reviewing your retirement savings from time to time to ensure you're still moving in the direction you want.

You don't need to check your balance every week. In fact, doing so may simply encourage unnecessary worry during periods when markets fluctuate. Instead, consider reviewing your progress periodically and making adjustments only when they genuinely support your long-term goals.

Retirement Is One Part of Your Financial Picture

While retirement savings are important, they are only one part of your overall financial plan.

Many people also build wealth through their home, investments, businesses, or other assets. Looking at your financial future as a whole often provides a clearer picture than focusing on one account alone. A balanced approach may provide greater flexibility throughout your life.

Give Yourself Choices

Ultimately, retirement planning isn't just about numbers. It's about creating opportunities. The opportunity to retire comfortably. The opportunity to spend more time with the people you care about. The opportunity to live with greater confidence and less financial stress. Those opportunities begin long before retirement itself. They begin with the decisions you make today.

Key Takeaways

- Retirement planning is about creating future choices, not simply stopping work.
- The earlier you begin, the more time your money has to grow.
- It is never too late to improve your retirement outlook.
- Many countries offer retirement savings accounts with valuable benefits.
- Reviewing your retirement plan from time to time helps keep you on track.
- Retirement savings should be viewed as part of your overall wealth-building strategy.

Take a Moment

Before moving on, ask yourself:

- Do I know how my retirement savings are invested?
- Am I contributing enough to support the retirement I hope to have?
- If I continue making the same financial decisions for the next 20 years, will I be happy with where they lead?
- What small change could I make today that my future self would appreciate?

Remember, retirement planning isn't about trying to predict the future.

It's about giving yourself more choices when the future arrives.

In the next chapter, we'll explore one of the most misunderstood areas of personal finance—tax—and why understanding the basics can help you keep more of the money you earn.

RETIREMENT GROWTH TIMELINE

THE POWER OF STARTING EARLY

The earlier you start, the more time your money has to grow.
Consistent contributions + time = financial freedom.

THE ASSUMPTIONS

- Invest $200 per month ($2,400 per year)
- Average annual return of 7%
- Contributions made at the end of each month

AGE 25 →	AGE 35 →	AGE 45 →	AGE 55 →	AGE 65
JUST STARTING	**MOMENTUM BUILDING**	**GROWTH ACCELERATES**	**COMPOUNDING IN FULL FORCE**	**FINANCIAL FREEDOM**
You're building a habit and planting the seed for your future.	Your money is growing, and compound interest is working for you.	Your money has more time to grow on top of itself.	Your money is working hard while you focus on your future.	Years of consistent investing can lead to the retirement you deserve.
TOTAL CONTRIBUTIONS **$24,000**	TOTAL CONTRIBUTIONS **$48,000**	TOTAL CONTRIBUTIONS **$72,000**	TOTAL CONTRIBUTIONS **$96,000**	TOTAL CONTRIBUTIONS **$120,000**

ESTIMATED VALUE **$37,611**	ESTIMATED VALUE **$98,087**	ESTIMATED VALUE **$205,726**	ESTIMATED VALUE **$404,033**	ESTIMATED VALUE **$748,252**
You're giving your money time to grow.	Small steps today create big change tomorrow.	You're halfway there. Stay consistent.	Time is your greatest advantage.	Your future self will thank you today.

THE KEY TAKEAWAY

Start early, stay consistent, and let time do the heavy lifting. The difference between starting at 25 and 35 could be hundreds of thousands of dollars.

REMEMBER

You don't have to be great at investing. You just need to start, stay consistent, and give your money time to grow.

Your future is built by what you do today.

Figures are for illustrative purposes only and not guarantees of future performance.

Chapter 10

Understanding Tax

Did You Know?

Paying less tax legally isn't about finding loopholes. It's about understanding the rules that already exist and making informed financial decisions within them. Many people pay more tax than necessary simply because they don't understand the basics.

Tax is a topic many people avoid. For some, it feels confusing. For others, it's simply something that happens automatically each payday. Yet understanding a few basic principles can make a meaningful difference to your long-term financial future.

This chapter isn't intended to make you a tax expert. Tax laws differ from country to country and change over time. Instead, the goal is to help you understand why tax matters and why learning the basics can help you keep more of the money you earn.

Tax Is Part of Financial Planning

Whenever you earn income, invest money, or sell certain assets, tax may become part of the picture.

Ignoring it doesn't make it disappear. Understanding it allows you to make more informed decisions.

Sometimes two investments produce exactly the same return before tax. After tax, however, one may leave you with significantly more money than the other. That's why successful wealth building isn't just about what you earn. It's also about what you keep.

Example

Imagine two investments.

Investment A earns an annual return of **8% before tax**.

Investment B earns **7.5% before tax**, but because of the way it is taxed in your circumstances, it leaves you with more money after tax.

Although Investment A appears to offer the higher return, Investment B could produce the better overall outcome.

When comparing investments, it's important to consider not only how much they earn, but also how much you keep after taxes and other costs.

Tax Planning Is Not Tax Avoidance

These terms are sometimes confused.

Tax planning means arranging your financial affairs within the law so you don't pay more tax than necessary.

Tax avoidance and tax evasion are different matters entirely.

This book encourages only lawful, ethical financial decision-making. Understanding available deductions, tax-efficient investment structures, and retirement savings opportunities can all form part of sensible financial planning. If you're unsure about your circumstances, seeking professional advice is often worthwhile.

Keep Good Records

One of the simplest financial habits you can develop is keeping accurate records.

Receipts. Statements. Investment records. Loan documents. Contribution records.

Good record keeping saves time, reduces stress, and makes it easier to understand your financial position. It may also help ensure you don't overlook deductions or other legitimate tax benefits that apply to your circumstances.

Understand Before You Invest

Some investments offer tax advantages. Others may have different tax consequences when they're sold or when they generate income. This doesn't mean you should invest purely to save tax.

An investment should still make financial sense on its own. However, understanding the tax implications before making a decision allows you to compare opportunities more accurately. Good financial decisions consider both the investment itself and the after-tax outcome.

Imagine This...

Emma and David each invest the same amount of money.

Both earn similar investment returns.

Emma spends a little time understanding the tax implications of her investment before she begins.

David focuses only on the expected return.

Years later, both have made money.

But Emma has kept more of what she earned because she understood how tax affected her investment decisions.

Sometimes building wealth isn't just about earning more.

It's also about keeping more.

Professional Advice Can Save Money

Many people see professional advice as an expense. Sometimes it is, other times, it becomes an investment. An experienced accountant or qualified financial adviser may identify opportunities or risks that you haven't considered.

That doesn't mean you need professional advice for every financial decision. But when your finances become more complex, seeking guidance may help you avoid costly mistakes.

Focus on the Bigger Picture

It's easy to become so focused on reducing tax that you lose sight of your overall financial goals. Paying less tax should never become the only reason for making an investment. The best financial decisions usually achieve both objectives. They make good financial sense and are tax-efficient where appropriate. Building wealth isn't about avoiding tax altogether. It's about making thoughtful decisions that leave more of your money working for you.

Key Takeaways

- Understanding basic tax principles can improve your long-term financial outcomes.
- Tax planning is different from tax avoidance or tax evasion.
- Good record keeping makes managing your finances much easier.
- Consider the after-tax outcome when comparing investments.
- Professional advice may become valuable as your financial situation grows more complex.
- Focus on building wealth, not simply reducing tax.

Take a Moment

Before moving on, ask yourself:

- Do I understand how tax affects my financial decisions?
- Am I keeping records that would make tax time easier?
- Have I ever chosen an investment without considering its tax implications?
- Would seeking professional advice help me make more informed financial decisions?

Remember, every dollar you legally keep is another dollar that can be saved, invested, or used to improve your future.

In the next chapter, we'll explore the role of financial professionals and how knowing when to seek expert advice can sometimes save far more than it costs.

TAX: BEFORE TAX vs AFTER TAX

FOCUS ON WHAT YOU KEEP, NOT JUST WHAT YOU EARN

It's not just about how much you earn on your investments, it's about how much you **keep after tax.**

BEFORE TAX

This is your investment return **before** any tax is paid.

EXAMPLE

You invest $10,000

Your return: 8% per year

After 1 year (before tax):

$10,800

VS.

AFTER TAX

This is your return **after** tax is paid.

EXAMPLE

Same investment: $10,000

Your return: 8% per year

Tax paid: 30% on gains

After 1 year (after tax):

$10,560

THE DIFFERENCE THAT MATTERS

INVESTMENT RETURN	BEFORE TAX (8% RETURN)	TAX PAID (30% ON GAINS)	AFTER TAX (WHAT YOU KEEP)
After 1 Year	$10,800	– $240	**$10,560**
After 10 Years	$21,589	– $3,477	**$18,112**
After 20 Years	$46,610	– $11,106	**$35,504**
After 30 Years	$100,627	– $27,885	**$72,742**

KEY POINT

The more tax you pay, the less you keep. Small differences in tax can create big differences over time.

TAX-EFFICIENT INVESTING TIPS

- Hold investments for the long term to reduce capital gains tax.
- Use tax-effective accounts where possible.
- Understand the tax implications of your investments.
- Consider income splitting and offsets where appropriate.
- Plan ahead. Good timing can save you tax.

THE TAKEAWAY

Before tax returns look good. After tax returns build your wealth.

Focus on what you keep, because that's what creates your future.

Chapter 11

Working With Financial Professionals

Did You Know?

Even the world's most successful athletes have coaches. Not because they can't perform on their own, but because an experienced guide can help them avoid mistakes, improve their skills, and reach their goals more effectively. Managing your finances can be much the same.

No one expects you to know everything about money. There may come a time when your financial situation becomes more complex than it once was. Perhaps you're buying your first home, starting a business, planning for retirement, managing an inheritance or making significant investments.

Seeking professional advice isn't a sign of weakness, it's a sign that you're making thoughtful decisions.

The right professional can help you understand your options, avoid costly mistakes, and make decisions with greater confidence.

Different Professionals Have Different Roles

Not all financial professionals do the same job.

An accountant may help you understand tax obligations, prepare tax returns, and keep your financial records in order.

A qualified financial adviser can help you develop a long-term financial plan, consider investment strategies, and prepare for retirement.

A mortgage broker may assist you in comparing home loan options.

A solicitor or lawyer may help with wills, estate planning, or legal matters relating to your finances.

Understanding who does what makes it easier to seek the right advice when you need it.

Ask Questions

It's easy to feel intimidated when speaking with professionals. Remember that you are the client. You have every right to ask questions until you understand the advice being given.

A good professional should be able to explain complex ideas in language that makes sense to you. If something isn't clear, ask again. There are no foolish questions when it comes to your financial future. Understanding your decisions is just as important as making them.

Imagine This...

Sophie receives an inheritance after the passing of a close relative.

Friends and family all have different opinions about what she should do with the money.

Some suggest buying property.

Others recommend investing in shares.

A few encourage her to start a business.

Rather than making a rushed decision, Sophie meets with a qualified financial professional to understand her options.

She doesn't receive a magical answer.

Instead, she gains something even more valuable - clarity.

With a better understanding of the advantages, risks, and long-term consequences of each option, she is able to make a decision that suits her own goals rather than simply following someone else's advice.

Sometimes the greatest value of professional advice isn't being told what to do.

It's gaining the confidence to make informed decisions yourself.

Beware of Free Financial Advice

Advice is everywhere.

Friends. Family. Work colleagues. Social media. Television. Podcasts.

While some advice can be helpful, not all of it applies to your situation.

What worked for someone else may not be right for you.

Be especially cautious of anyone promising guaranteed returns, quick riches, or "can't lose" investments.

If something sounds too good to be true, it usually deserves a closer look.

A Good Adviser Helps You Learn

The best financial professionals don't simply tell you what to do.

They help you understand why.

Over time, this knowledge allows you to become more confident in managing your own finances.

A good adviser should educate as well as guide.

Their goal should be to help you make informed decisions—not to make you dependent on them.

You Are Still Responsible

Even when you receive professional advice, the final decisions remain yours.

Take the time to understand recommendations before acting on them.

Read important documents. Ask questions. Consider whether the advice aligns with your values, goals, and circumstances.

No one will ever care about your financial future as much as you do.

Professional advice is there to support your decisions—not replace them.

Key Takeaways

- Financial professionals can provide valuable guidance as your finances become more complex.
- Different professionals have different areas of expertise.
- Never be afraid to ask questions until you understand the advice you receive.
- Be cautious of financial advice from unqualified or unreliable sources.
- A good adviser should help you learn, not simply tell you what to do.
- You remain responsible for the financial decisions you make.

Take a Moment

Before moving on, ask yourself:

- Do I know when I should seek professional financial advice?
- Am I comfortable asking questions when I don't understand something?
- Where do I currently get most of my financial information?
- Am I relying on opinions, or am I making informed decisions based on trustworthy advice?

Remember, asking for guidance doesn't mean giving up control.

The best advice helps you make better decisions while keeping your future firmly in your own hands.

In the next chapter, we'll look at one of the most important—and often overlooked—parts of building wealth: protecting what you've worked so hard to achieve.

FINANCIAL PROFESSIONALS

Who Can Help?

You don't have to do everything on your own.
The right professionals can help you make better decisions, save money, reduce risk, and build your wealth.

ACCOUNTANT

Experts in taxes, numbers, and financial reporting.

They can help you:

- Lodge your tax return
- Minimise tax legally
- Manage deductions
- Structure your business or investments

Best for: Tax, numbers, and compliance.

FINANCIAL ADVISER

Experts in financial planning and long-term strategy.

They can help you:

- Create a personalised financial plan
- Grow and protect your wealth
- Plan for retirement
- Set and achieve your financial goals

Best for: Long-term planning and strategy.

MORTGAGE BROKER

Experts in home loans and borrowing solutions.

They can help you:

- Compare home loan options
- Find competitive rates
- Simplify the loan process
- Save you time and potentially money

Best for: Home loans and refinancing.

LAWYER

Experts in the law and protecting your interests.

They can help you:

- Review contracts
- Help with estate planning
- Set up trusts
- Protect your assets
- Navigate legal issues

Best for: Legal advice and asset protection.

BANK

Provides financial products and daily banking services.

They can help you:

- Transaction and savings accounts
- Home loans and personal loans
- Credit cards
- Term deposits and investment options

Best for: Banking and finance products.

INSURANCE ADVISER

Experts in protecting you and what matters most.

They can help you:

- Life insurance
- Income protection
- Total and permanent disability (TPD)
- Trauma and health insurance
- Protect your family and income

Best for: Insurance and risk protection.

HOW THEY WORK TOGETHER

Each professional plays a different role, but together they help you build a stronger financial future.

THE TAKEAWAY

You don't need to work with all of them at once. Start with who you need most right now.

The right advice at the right time can save you money, reduce stress, and help you reach your goals faster.

REMEMBER: Ask questions, understand the advice, and choose professionals you trust. Good advice is an investment in your future.

Chapter 12

Protecting Your Wealth

Did You Know?

Building wealth is only half the challenge. Protecting it is just as important. A single unexpected event—a serious illness, natural disaster, legal dispute, or lack of planning—can have significant financial consequences if you're unprepared.

Many people spend years learning how to earn more money. Some learn how to save and invest. Far fewer spend time thinking about how to protect what they've built. Protecting your wealth isn't about expecting the worst. It’s about preparing for life's uncertainties so that one unexpected event doesn't undo years of hard work. No one can predict exactly what the future holds, but everyone can take sensible steps to reduce unnecessary financial risk.

Build an Emergency Fund

One of the simplest ways to protect yourself is by having an emergency fund. Life rarely goes exactly as planned. Cars break down, homes need repairs, medical expenses arise. Employment situations can change.

Without savings set aside, unexpected costs often end up on credit cards or loans, creating additional financial pressure. An emergency fund provides a financial buffer during difficult times. It may not remove the problem, but it can give you more time, more choices, and greater peace of mind.

Insurance Has a Purpose

Insurance isn't exciting. In fact, many people hope they'll never need to use it. That's exactly the point.

Insurance is designed to help protect you from financial losses that would otherwise be difficult to recover from. Depending on your circumstances, this may include insurance for your home, vehicle, health, income, business, or life. The right type and amount of insurance will differ from person to person. Rather than viewing insurance as a wasted expense, think of it as part of your overall financial protection plan.

Keep Your Financial Information Organised

Knowing where your important financial documents are can save considerable stress during difficult times.

This might include:

- Bank account details
- Investment records
- Insurance policies
- Loan documents

- Property information
- Wills and estate planning documents

Keeping these organised—and ensuring someone you trust knows how to access essential information if necessary—can make life much easier for your family.

Imagine This...

Robert has spent many years building his savings and investments.

He keeps important documents in different places throughout the house.

Some are stored digitally.

Others are in drawers he rarely opens.

When Robert unexpectedly becomes ill, his family struggles to find important information.

Accounts are difficult to locate.

Insurance details are missing.

Simple tasks become stressful during an already emotional time.

His neighbour, Helen, has a folder containing all her important financial information, along with clear instructions about where key documents are stored.

When an unexpected situation arises, her family knows exactly where to begin.

Sometimes protecting your wealth has nothing to do with earning more money. It's about being organised so that you and your family can easily manage your finances when life doesn't go as planned.

Plan for the Unexpected

None of us enjoys thinking about illness or death. Yet planning ahead is one of the kindest things we can do for the people we care about.

Having an up-to-date will, reviewing beneficiaries on important accounts where applicable, and discussing your wishes with trusted family members can prevent unnecessary confusion and conflict later. These conversations may feel uncomfortable today, but they often provide reassurance tomorrow.

Continue Reviewing Your Financial Life

Protection isn't something you do once. As your life changes, your financial protection should change too. Marriage, children, buying a home or starting a business. Approaching retirement.

Each stage of life may require you to review your savings, insurance, investments, and legal documents. A simple annual review can help ensure your financial plan continues to match your circumstances.

Peace of Mind Is Valuable

Financial success isn't measured only by how much money you have. It's also measured by how secure you feel. Knowing you've prepared for unexpected events allows you to focus more on living your life and less on worrying about what might happen. While no plan can remove every risk, thoughtful preparation can make many challenges easier to manage.

Key Takeaways

- Protecting your wealth is just as important as building it.
- An emergency fund provides valuable financial security during unexpected events.
- Insurance helps protect against significant financial losses.
- Keeping financial documents organised can save your family unnecessary stress.
- Estate planning and reviewing important documents are part of responsible financial planning.
- Regularly reviewing your financial protection helps keep your plan up to date.

Take a Moment

Before moving on, ask yourself:

- Could I manage an unexpected financial emergency without borrowing money?
- Are my important financial documents organised and easy to find?
- Have I reviewed my insurance and legal documents recently?
- If something happened to me tomorrow, would my family know where to find the information they need?

Remember, protecting your wealth isn't about living in fear.

It's about preparing wisely so that life's unexpected moments don't derail the future you've worked hard to build.

In the next chapter, we'll explore passive income and why earning money doesn't always require trading more of your time for more income.

PROTECTING YOUR WEALTH

THE FINANCIAL PROTECTION PYRAMID

Wealth isn't just about earning and growing your money.
It's also about protecting it.
Use this pyramid as your guide to building a strong
and secure financial future.

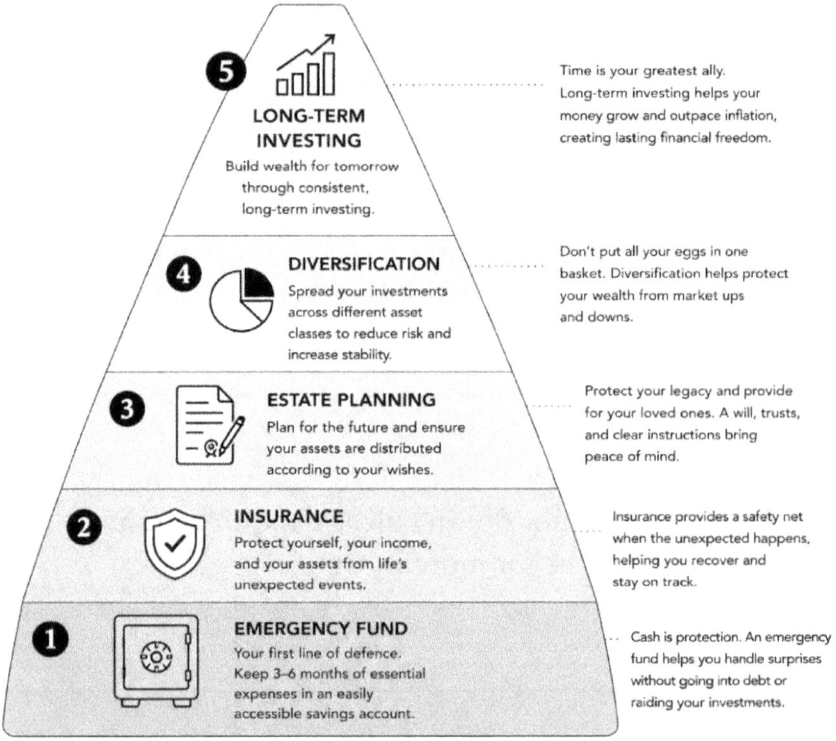

WHY THIS PYRAMID WORKS

- ✔ Build a strong foundation first.
- ✔ Protect what you have.
- ✔ Plan for the unexpected.
- ✔ Grow your wealth wisely.
- ✔ Secure your financial future.

THE TAKEAWAY

True wealth is built on protection as well as growth.

Build each layer with care, and your financial future will be stronger, no matter what life brings.

REMEMBER: Protecting your wealth today gives you the freedom to enjoy your life tomorrow.

Chapter 13

Passive Income Explained

Did You Know?

Passive income doesn't mean making money without doing any work. In most cases, it requires time, effort, or money upfront. The goal is to create income that continues to flow with less ongoing effort than earning a regular wage.

For most people, earning money means exchanging time for income. You go to work, you complete your tasks and you receive a pay cheque. There is nothing wrong with this. In fact, it is how most people begin building their financial future.

The challenge is that there are only so many hours in a day. If your income depends entirely on your time, there is a limit to how much you can earn. Passive income aims to reduce that limitation. It is money that continues to come in after the initial work or investment has been made.

While many people dream of passive income, it is important to understand that it is rarely effortless. Most passive income streams require planning, patience, and ongoing management.

Passive Doesn't Mean No Work

One of the biggest myths about passive income is that it allows you to make money while doing nothing. In reality, most passive income begins with considerable effort. Writing a book takes time, building an investment portfolio takes discipline.

Buying an investment property requires planning and ongoing responsibilities. Creating an online course may take weeks or months before it is ready to sell. The work usually comes first. The income follows later.

Common Sources of Passive Income

Passive income can come from many different sources.

Some examples include:

- Dividends from shares.
- Income from ETFs that distribute earnings.
- Rental income from investment properties.
- Royalties from books, music, photography, or other creative work.
- Income from online courses or digital products.
- Interest earned on savings or certain investments.
- Businesses that continue operating without requiring your constant involvement.

Some of these income streams require significant money to begin.

Others require more time than money.

There is no single path that suits everyone.

Example

Monthly Passive Income

Dividends – **$80**

Interest – **$40**

Vending machine – **$250**

Reselling items – **$180**

Total Monthly Passive Income: $550

None of these income streams is life-changing on its own. However, when combined, they provide an additional $550 each month. Over time, building several smaller income streams can create greater financial security and reduce reliance on a single source of income.

Reselling items – **$180**

Small Streams Can Become Bigger Rivers

Many people believe they need one large source of passive income.

In reality, wealth is often built by combining several smaller income streams over time.

A little dividend income. A little interest. A small royalty payment. A modest rental return.

Individually, these amounts may seem insignificant.

Together, they can gradually become an important part of your financial picture.

> **Imagine This...**
>
> Ben and Lucy both work full-time.
>
> Ben spends nearly every extra dollar he earns.
>
> Lucy saves consistently for several years before buying two vending machines in busy locations.
>
> The machines require occasional restocking and maintenance, but they continue generating income each month.
>
> Lucy still works full-time, but part of her income no longer depends entirely on the hours she works each week.
>
> Passive income often starts small. The important thing is creating something that has the potential to continue earning money long after the initial effort has been made.

Passive Income Takes Patience

Many passive income streams grow slowly. They often require years of consistent effort before the results become noticeable. This is one reason many people give up too soon. They expect immediate returns. Instead, they find slow progress.

Building passive income is much like planting a tree. The greatest growth often happens after years of patient care.

Choose Income Streams That Suit You

Not every passive income opportunity will suit your interests, skills, or financial circumstances. Someone with savings may choose investments. Someone with specialist knowledge may create educational content. A creative person may write books, compose music, or license artwork. An entrepreneur may build a business that eventually operates with less day-to-day involvement.

There is no perfect approach. The best passive income strategy is one that matches your abilities, goals, and willingness to commit for the long term.

Passive Income Supports Financial Freedom

Passive income does not guarantee wealth. Nor does it replace the importance of earning, saving, and investing wisely. Instead, it can become another source of financial stability.

Over time, additional income streams may provide greater flexibility, reduce financial pressure, and create more choices about how you spend your time. That is the real value of passive income.

It gives your money—and sometimes your earlier efforts—the opportunity to continue working alongside you.

Key Takeaways

- Passive income usually requires work or investment before it generates ongoing income.
- Most passive income streams grow gradually rather than overnight.
- There are many different ways to create passive income.
- Multiple small income streams can become significant over time.
- Choose passive income opportunities that match your skills, interests, and financial goals.
- Passive income can provide greater financial flexibility and more choices in the future.

Take a Moment

Before moving on, ask yourself:

- Do I currently have any source of passive income?
- What skills or assets do I already have that could create income in the future?
- Am I willing to invest time now for the possibility of earning income later?

- Which passive income opportunity interests me the most?

Remember, passive income isn't about getting rich quickly.

It's about creating opportunities for your time, money, and effort to continue working for you long into the future.

In the next chapter, we'll explore the many different ways money can work for you and why building several income streams can create greater financial resilience.

MULTIPLE INCOME STREAMS

One job pays the bills. Multiple streams build wealth and freedom.

The goal is not just to earn more, but to create income from different sources so your life is not dependent on just one.

Diversify your income. Secure your future.

When one stream slows down, your other streams keep you moving forward.

More streams. More security. More freedom.

Chapter 14

Different Ways Money Can Work for You

Did You Know?

There are only so many hours in a day. No matter how hard you work, your time is limited. One of the most important financial lessons you can learn is how to make your money work alongside you instead of relying only on your own efforts.

When most people think about earning money, they think about working. You exchange your time, skills, and effort for a pay cheque. For many people, this is where their financial journey begins. But over time, the goal should be to gradually rely less on your time alone.

As you save, invest, and build assets, your money can begin contributing to your financial future as well. This doesn't happen overnight. It happens gradually through consistent decisions made over many years.

Every Dollar Has a Job

Imagine every dollar you earn is an employee. You can spend it immediately. Or you can give it a job. Some dollars might earn interest. Some may buy shares that pay dividends.

Others may help purchase property that generates rental income. Some may fund a business or create a product that earns money for years to come. The more dollars you put to work, the harder your financial team begins working for you.

Income Can Come From Many Places

Many financially secure people don't rely on just one source of income.

Instead, they gradually build several.

These might include:

- Employment income.
- Business income.
- Dividend income.
- Rental income.
- Interest income.
- Royalties.
- Retirement income.
- Income from digital products or online businesses.

Not everyone will have all of these.

And that's perfectly fine.

The goal isn't to collect every possible income stream.

It's to reduce the risk of depending entirely on one.

Example

Sarah earns:

- Salary – $75,000
- Dividends – $1,500
- Vending Machine – $4,000
- Reselling – $3,000

If Sarah loses her job, she still has other sources of income while she looks for new employment

Diversification Creates Resilience

Imagine a table with only one leg. If that leg breaks, the entire table falls. Now imagine a table with several strong legs. If one becomes weaker, the table remains standing. Your income can work in much the same way.

If one source of income is interrupted, other sources may continue supporting your financial goals. Diversification doesn't remove risk completely. But it often reduces the impact of unexpected setbacks.

Imagine This...

Anthony has worked for the same company for twenty years.

His salary is his only source of income.

When the company restructures, he suddenly finds himself without a job.

At the same time, Michelle also loses her job.

Like Anthony, she has employment income.

But over the years she has also built a small investment portfolio, receives modest royalties from a book she wrote, and earns a little income from an online course.

None of those income streams replace her salary.

Together, however, they provide enough breathing room to reduce financial stress while she looks for her next opportunity.

Building multiple income streams isn't about becoming wealthy overnight.

It's about creating greater stability when life takes an unexpected turn.

Let Your Income Grow With You

Most people don't build several income streams all at once. They build them gradually. Perhaps you begin with regular employment, later, you start investing. Years later, you purchase an investment property.

Eventually, you might start a small business, buy an investment property, purchase a vending machine, begin buying and reselling products, or invest in another income-producing asset. Each step builds on the one before it. Financial freedom is often the result of many small decisions rather than one extraordinary event.

Your Greatest Investment Is Still You

While this chapter focuses on making money work for you, never forget that your greatest asset is often your ability to learn. New skills can increase your earning potential. Experience can create opportunities. Knowledge can help you recognise possibilities that others overlook.

Investing in yourself through education, training, reading, or developing new skills may produce returns that last a lifetime.

Build Slowly and Consistently

It's easy to compare yourself with people who appear financially successful.

What you don't always see are the years of steady work that came before their success. Building wealth rarely happens overnight. It grows through patience, consistency, learning and making thoughtful decisions over many years.

The important thing isn't how quickly you begin - It's that you begin.

Key Takeaways

- Your time is limited, but your money can continue working long after you earn it.
- Every dollar can either be spent or put to work.

- Building multiple income streams can improve financial resilience.
- Diversification helps reduce reliance on a single source of income.
- Investing in yourself can be one of the best financial decisions you ever make.
- Wealth is usually built gradually through consistent action over time.

Take a Moment

Before moving on, ask yourself:

- Where does my income currently come from?
- Am I relying too heavily on one source of income?
- What additional income stream could I realistically begin building over the next few years?
- How could investing in my own knowledge or skills improve my financial future?

Remember, every income stream you build today has the potential to provide greater freedom and security tomorrow.

In the next chapter, we'll explore one of the most important factors in financial success—your mindset—and how the way you think about money can influence the decisions you make throughout your life.

Chapter 15

The Wealth Mindset

Did You Know?

Two people can earn exactly the same income and end up in completely different financial positions. Often, the difference isn't how much they earn—it's the decisions they make consistently over time.

When people hear the phrase *wealth mindset*, they sometimes imagine positive thinking alone will make them rich. It won't. A healthy wealth mindset isn't about wishing for success or believing money will somehow appear.

It's about developing habits, attitudes, and behaviours that support good financial decisions over the long term. The way you think about money influences the choices you make every day. Those choices, repeated over months and years, shape your financial future.

Think Long Term

Many financial decisions involve choosing between what feels good today and what benefits you tomorrow. That doesn't mean you should never enjoy your money. Life is meant to be lived.

But learning to balance today's enjoyment with tomorrow's security is one of the most valuable financial skills you can develop.

People who build wealth often become comfortable delaying some rewards so they can create greater opportunities later.

Focus on Progress, Not Perfection

One of the biggest reasons people give up is because they believe they need to get everything right from the beginning. They don't. Everyone makes financial mistakes.

The important thing is learning from them and continuing to move forward. Missing a month of saving doesn't mean you've failed. Making one poor investment doesn't mean you'll never succeed. Progress is built through consistency, not perfection.

Avoid Comparing Yourself With Others

It has never been easier to compare your life with someone else's. Social media often shows expensive holidays, luxury cars, large homes, and apparent financial success.

What it rarely shows are debts, financial stress, sacrifices, or years of steady work behind those achievements.

Comparing your financial journey with someone else's can lead to unnecessary frustration and poor decisions. The only comparison that truly matters is whether you're making better financial decisions than you were yesterday.

Imagine This...

Nathan and Olivia both receive a pay rise.

Nathan immediately upgrades his car and increases his spending because he feels he can now afford more.

Olivia enjoys a small celebration but decides to save and invest most of her additional income.

Neither decision changes their lives overnight.

But over the next ten years, Olivia's extra savings continue growing through investment returns and compound growth, while Nathan's higher spending becomes his new normal.

Small decisions repeated consistently often produce very different outcomes.

Keep Learning

The financial world changes.

New opportunities emerge.

Markets rise and fall.

Technology evolves.

The people who continue learning place themselves in a stronger position to recognise opportunities and avoid unnecessary risks.

You don't need to become an expert. Reading books, listening to reliable podcasts, attending seminars, or following trusted financial educators can gradually increase your confidence and understanding.

Knowledge is one of the few investments that can continue paying dividends throughout your life.

Build Habits That Last

Building wealth is rarely the result of one extraordinary decision. More often, it comes from ordinary habits repeated consistently.

Saving regularly. Avoiding unnecessary debt. Investing consistently. Reviewing your finances. Living within your means. Learning continuously.

Individually, these habits may seem small.

Together, they can shape your financial future.

Your Future Self Is Counting on You

Every financial decision you make today has the potential to influence your future. Your future self cannot change the choices you make today. But today's decisions can make tomorrow's opportunities greater.

Every dollar saved. Every investment made. Every skill learned. Every good habit developed.

These are gifts you give to the person you will become.

Key Takeaways

- A wealth mindset is built through habits and thoughtful decisions, not wishful thinking.
- Long-term thinking often leads to better financial outcomes.
- Progress matters more than perfection.
- Avoid comparing your financial journey with others.
- Continue learning throughout your life.
- Small habits repeated consistently can produce remarkable results over time.

Take a Moment

Before moving on, ask yourself:

- What financial habits am I strengthening each day?
- Do I make decisions with my future in mind?
- Am I comparing my progress with others instead of focusing on my own journey?
- What is one financial habit I could improve starting today?

Remember, building wealth isn't about making one perfect decision.

It's about making good decisions consistently over many years.

In the next chapter, we'll explore some of the most common financial mistakes people make—and how avoiding them can sometimes be just as valuable as making a great investment.

Chapter 16

Mistakes That Cost People a Fortune

Did You Know?

Some of the biggest financial losses don't happen because people make one terrible decision. They happen because small mistakes are repeated over many years. Avoiding costly mistakes can sometimes be just as powerful as making great investments.

Throughout this book, we've explored ways to grow your money. We've discussed saving, investing, managing debt, building passive income, and developing habits that support long-term success. But building wealth isn't only about doing the right things. It's also about avoiding the wrong ones.

No one makes perfect financial decisions all the time. Everyone makes mistakes. The goal isn't perfection. The goal is recognising mistakes early, learning from them, and making better decisions moving forward.

Waiting for the Perfect Time

One of the most expensive financial mistakes is waiting.

Waiting until you earn more.

Waiting until markets settle.

Waiting until you know everything.

Waiting until life feels less busy.

The perfect time rarely arrives.

Meanwhile, time continues passing.

Starting with small, consistent actions today is usually far more valuable than waiting for ideal circumstances that may never come.

Lifestyle Inflation

As income increases, spending often increases too.

A larger home.

A newer car.

More expensive holidays.

Higher monthly subscriptions.

Enjoying the rewards of your hard work is important. But if every pay rise disappears into higher spending, building wealth becomes much more difficult. Whenever your income grows, consider allowing part of that increase to improve your future as well as your lifestyle.

Trying to Get Rich Quickly

Stories of overnight success attract attention. In reality, lasting wealth is usually built slowly. Be cautious of anyone promising guaranteed profits, secret investment strategies, or extraordinary returns with little or no risk. If building wealth were truly that easy, everyone would already be doing it.

Slow, steady progress may not be exciting, but it has helped many people achieve lasting financial security.

Imagine This...

James hears about an investment that promises to double his money within a year.

Several friends are excited and tell him he needs to act quickly before he misses out.

David hears about the same opportunity.

Instead of rushing in, he asks questions.

He researches the investment.

He considers the risks.

When he still isn't comfortable, he decides not to invest.

Months later, the investment fails, and many people lose their savings.

Sometimes the best financial decision is the one you choose not to make.

Ignoring Small Expenses

Many people focus only on large purchases. But small, regular expenses can quietly add up over time.

Subscriptions you no longer use, bank fees, interest on unnecessary debt or impulse purchases.

None of these may seem significant on their own. Together, however, they can quietly reduce the amount available for saving and investing. Reviewing your spending occasionally doesn't mean removing everything you enjoy. It simply means making sure your money is going where you genuinely want it to go.

Failing to Keep Learning

The financial world changes. New opportunities appear; new risks emerge. People who stop learning often rely on outdated information or assumptions.

You don't need to become an expert. But remaining curious and continuing to improve your financial knowledge can help you make better decisions throughout your life.

Believing It's Too Late

Perhaps the saddest financial mistake of all is believing you've missed your chance.

Many people tell themselves:

"I'm too old."

"I should have started years ago."

"I've made too many mistakes."

The truth is that you cannot change yesterday.

But you can change what happens next. Every positive financial decision you make from this point forward has the potential to improve your future. It is never too late to begin. As we've said throughout this book, the best time to start may have been years ago. The second-best time is today.

Key Takeaways

- Small financial mistakes repeated over time can become very costly.
- Waiting for the perfect moment often delays progress unnecessarily.
- Lifestyle inflation can prevent long-term wealth building.
- Be cautious of opportunities that promise quick or guaranteed riches.
- Regularly reviewing your spending helps ensure your money reflects your priorities.
- It is never too late to improve your financial future.

Take a Moment

Before moving on, ask yourself:

- Which financial mistake am I most likely to make?
- Have I delayed important financial decisions because I was waiting for the "right" time?

- Has my spending increased as my income has grown?
- What is one mistake I can avoid from today onwards?

Remember, building wealth isn't about never making mistakes.

It's about recognising them, learning from them, and continuing to move forward with confidence.

In the next chapter, we'll bring everything together by creating a practical 10-year wealth plan that turns the ideas in this book into achievable action.

Chapter 17

Your 10-Year Wealth Plan

> **Did You Know?**
>
> Most people dramatically overestimate what they can achieve in one year. At the same time, they often underestimate what they can achieve in ten. Small, consistent actions repeated over a decade can completely change your financial future.

Throughout this book, we've explored the principles of building wealth. Saving, investing, managing debt, planning for retirement, creating passive income, and developing healthy financial habits.

Now it's time to bring those ideas together. A ten-year plan doesn't need to predict every detail of your future. Life will change. Your income may change. Your goals may change. The purpose of a long-term plan isn't to predict the future perfectly. It's to give yourself direction.

Know Where You Are Today

Every journey begins with understanding your starting point. Take an honest look at your current financial situation. How much do you earn? How much do you spend? Do you have savings? Do you have debt? Are you already investing?

You cannot create an effective plan without first understanding where you are today. There is no reason to feel embarrassed if your finances aren't where you'd like them to be. Everyone starts somewhere.

Decide Where You Want to Be

Once you know where you are, think about where you would like to be in ten years.

Perhaps you hope to:

- Own your own home.
- Pay off your mortgage.
- Become debt free.
- Build an investment portfolio.
- Create passive income.
- Save for your children's education.
- Retire comfortably.
- Start your own business.

Your goals do not need to look like anyone else's.

Your wealth plan should reflect the life you want to build.

Break Big Goals Into Small Steps

Large financial goals can sometimes feel overwhelming. The secret is breaking them into smaller actions. If you want to save $100,000, don't focus only on the final number. Focus on today's contribution.

If you want to become debt free, concentrate on paying a little more each month. If you want to invest, begin with an amount you can comfortably afford. Small actions, repeated consistently, often achieve far more than occasional bursts of motivation.

Imagine This...

Rachel and Michael both dream of becoming financially secure. Rachel spends years talking about what she hopes to do one day.

Michael writes down his goals. He decides how much he wants to save each month. He sets up automatic transfers into his savings and investment accounts. He reviews his progress once each year and makes small adjustments along the way.

Ten years later, life hasn't gone exactly as planned for either of them. Both have experienced unexpected expenses and setbacks. But Michael has made steady progress because he turned good intentions into consistent action.

A simple plan followed consistently will usually achieve more than a perfect plan that is never started.

Review Your Plan Regularly

A ten-year plan should not be locked away in a drawer. Review it regularly. Celebrate your progress. Adjust your goals as your circumstances change. Life rarely follows a straight path. Your financial plan should be flexible enough to grow with you.

Celebrate Small Wins

Building wealth is a long journey. Waiting ten years before celebrating success can make the process feel overwhelming. Instead, recognise the smaller milestones along the way.

Paying off a credit card. Saving your first emergency fund. Making your first investment. Paying off your car loan. Reaching your first $10,000 in savings. Each milestone is evidence that your efforts are moving you closer to your larger goals.

Remember Why You Started

Money is a tool. The purpose of building wealth isn't simply to watch numbers grow. It's about creating opportunities, reducing stress, providing security for yourself and the people you love, and giving yourself greater freedom to choose how you spend your time.

Whenever motivation begins to fade, remind yourself why your financial goals matter.

That purpose will often carry you further than motivation alone.

Key Takeaways

- A long-term financial plan provides direction, even when life changes.
- Understanding your current financial position is the first step.
- Break large goals into small, achievable actions.
- Review your plan regularly and adjust it when necessary.
- Celebrate progress along the way.
- Remember that wealth is a tool for creating the life you want.

Take a Moment

Before moving on, ask yourself:

- Where would I like to be financially in ten years?
- What is the most important financial goal I want to achieve?
- What small action could I take this week to move closer to that goal?
- How will I measure my progress over time?

Remember, you don't need to have everything figured out today.

You simply need to begin and keep moving forward.

In the next chapter, we'll look even further ahead and explore how thinking twenty years into the future can help you make better financial decisions today.

Chapter 18

Your 20-Year Wealth Plan

Did You Know?

Many of the world's most successful investors didn't become wealthy because they made one brilliant decision. They became wealthy because they consistently made good decisions over many decades. Time is one of the greatest advantages you can have when building wealth.

Ten years is enough time to make remarkable financial progress. Twenty years can be life-changing.

By now, you have explored the principles of saving, investing, managing debt, protecting your wealth, creating additional income streams, and developing habits that support long-term success. The next step is to think even further ahead.

When you begin making decisions with your future twenty years in mind, many short-term distractions become less important. You begin asking different questions. Not, "Can I afford this today?" But, "Will this decision help create the future I want?"

Imagine Your Future

Take a moment to picture your life twenty years from now. Where do you want to live? Will you still be working? If so, will it be because you have to—or because you choose to? What experiences would you like to have? What security would you like to provide for your family?

Thinking about the future gives your financial decisions a purpose. Without a destination, it becomes difficult to choose the right path.

Build a Life, Not Just a Bank Balance

Money is important. But money is not the goal. The goal is creating a life that reflects your values.

Perhaps financial success means spending more time with your family. Perhaps it means travelling. Helping your children. Supporting causes you care about. Starting a business. Working fewer hours.

Everyone's definition of success is different. Your financial plan should support the life you want—not someone else's version of success.

Stay Flexible

No twenty-year plan will unfold exactly as expected. Careers change. Families grow. Unexpected opportunities appear. Challenges arise. Markets rise and fall. Life happens.

That doesn't mean planning is pointless. It simply means your plan should evolve as your life evolves. A clear direction is more important than predicting every step.

Imagine This...

Daniel and Sophie are both in their thirties. Daniel spends time each year reviewing his financial goals. When his income increases, he saves and invests part of the extra money. When unexpected setbacks occur, he adjusts his plan and keeps moving forward.

Sophie rarely thinks beyond the next holiday or major purchase. She assumes there will always be time to start planning later.

Twenty years pass more quickly than either of them expected. Neither life has been perfect. Both have experienced challenges. But Daniel has gradually built financial security because he made long-term planning part of his life rather than something he intended to do someday.

The future is shaped less by one extraordinary decision than by thousands of ordinary decisions made consistently over time.

Leave a Legacy

Building wealth is not only about improving your own life. For many people, it is also about creating opportunities for others.

Perhaps you hope to help your children. Support your grandchildren. Give to charity. Leave behind a thriving business. Or simply ensure your family has greater financial security than you did.

Wealth can become a gift that extends far beyond your own lifetime.

Success Is Measured in More Than Money

As your financial position improves, remember that true wealth includes far more than the balance in your bank account. Good health. Strong relationships. Meaningful work. Peace of mind. Time with the people you love.

Money can support these things, but it cannot replace them.

A successful financial life is one that helps you enjoy a successful life overall.

Keep Moving Forward

You don't need to become wealthy overnight. You don't need to know everything before you begin. You simply need to continue moving forward.

Save consistently. Invest wisely. Keep learning. Review your progress. Adapt when life changes.

These habits, repeated year after year, have the power to transform your future.

Key Takeaways

- Twenty years of consistent financial decisions can produce extraordinary results.
- Build a financial plan that supports the life you want to live.
- Stay flexible and adjust your plan as life changes.
- Wealth can create opportunities not only for you but also for future generations.
- True success includes health, relationships, purpose, and peace of mind.
- Consistency over decades is more powerful than short bursts of motivation.

Take a Moment

Before moving on, ask yourself:

- What do I want my life to look like twenty years from now?
- What financial decisions can I make today to move closer to that future?
- What kind of legacy would I like to leave?
- Am I building wealth to impress others, or to create the life that truly matters to me?

Remember, your future is created one decision at a time.

> Every thoughtful choice you make today is an investment in the life you hope to live tomorrow.

In our final chapter, we'll bring together everything you've learned in this book and leave you with one simple message: building wealth is possible for ordinary people who are willing to begin, remain consistent, and keep moving forward.

Chapter 19

The Best Time to Begin Is Today

Did You Know?

The journey to financial security rarely begins with a large inheritance, a winning lottery ticket, or a perfect investment. More often, it begins with one simple decision: to start.

If you've read this far, you've already taken an important step. You've invested your time in learning about money. That alone puts you ahead of many people who spend years hoping their financial situation will improve without ever changing the way they think about it.

Throughout this book, we've explored many different aspects of building wealth. We've discussed saving, investing, debt, property, retirement planning, passive income, protecting your wealth, and developing habits that support long-term success.

While each chapter focused on a different topic, they all point towards the same simple truth. Building wealth isn't about finding one secret. It's about making good decisions consistently over time.

You Don't Need to Be Perfect

Perhaps there were moments in this book when you recognised mistakes you've made. Maybe you've spent more than you should have. Delayed investing. Accumulated debt. Missed opportunities. Almost everyone has.

The purpose of this book was never to make you feel guilty about the past. The past cannot be changed. But your future is still being written. Every positive decision you make from today onwards has the potential to improve your financial future.

Small Actions Create Big Results

Many people never begin because they think their first step is too small to matter. A small amount invested. An extra payment on a loan. One unnecessary subscription cancelled. The first contribution to an emergency fund.

Each action may seem insignificant on its own. But wealth is rarely built through one extraordinary event. It is built through hundreds—often thousands—of ordinary decisions repeated consistently over many years. Never underestimate the power of small actions.

Imagine This...

Two friends leave this book with exactly the same knowledge. Emma closes the book, feels inspired, and tells herself she'll begin "when the time is right." Michael closes the book and spends thirty minutes making a simple plan.

He sets up an automatic transfer into his savings account. He reviews his monthly spending. He chooses one long-term financial goal and writes it down.

Neither person's life changes overnight. But one has taken the first step. Years later, that single decision has grown into many others. Knowledge creates opportunity. Action creates results.

Keep Learning

No single book can teach you everything about money. Nor should it. Financial learning is a lifelong journey. Continue reading. Continue asking questions. Continue improving your understanding.

The more you learn, the more confident you'll become in making financial decisions that support the life you want.

Wealth Is About Freedom

Throughout history, people have defined wealth in many different ways. For some, it means financial independence. For others, it means security. Time with family. The freedom to choose meaningful work. Helping others. Leaving a legacy.

Whatever wealth means to you, remember that money is a tool. Its greatest value lies in the opportunities it creates. Use it wisely.

A Final Thought

If there is one idea I hope stays with you after reading this book, it is this: You do not need to earn the highest income. You do not need to know everything. You do not need to make perfect financial decisions. You simply need to begin.

Save what you can. Invest what you can. Learn whenever you can. Stay patient. Stay consistent. And keep moving forward.

Over time, those ordinary decisions have the potential to create an extraordinary future.

Key Takeaways

- Building wealth is the result of consistent decisions rather than one perfect opportunity.
- Your past financial mistakes do not define your future.
- Small actions, repeated over time, can produce remarkable results.
- Continue learning throughout your life.
- Wealth is a tool that creates freedom, opportunity, and security.
- The most important step is simply to begin.

Take a Moment

As you close this book, ask yourself:

- What is the very first financial action I will take after finishing this book?
- What habit will I commit to improving over the next month?
- What kind of financial future do I want to create for myself and the people I care about?
- If I remain consistent over the next twenty years, where could today's decision take me?

Remember...

The best time to start may have been years ago.

The second-best time is today.

Your future begins with the decision you make next.

Thank you for allowing me to be part of your financial journey.

I wish you every success in building a future filled with confidence, opportunity, and lasting financial security.

YOUR 10-YEAR WEALTH ROADMAP

A DECADE OF SMART DECISIONS CAN CREATE GENERATIONAL WEALTH.

Stay consistent, keep learning, and let time work in your favour.

	FOCUS	KEY ACTIONS	OUTCOME
YEAR 1	**BUILD YOUR FOUNDATION** Create strong habits and get your finances in order.	• Track your income and expenses • Build an emergency fund (3–6 months of expenses) • Pay off high-interest debt • Create a budget and stick to it • Start investing – even small amounts	You gain control of your money and build financial confidence.
YEARS 2-3	**BUILD MOMENTUM** Strengthen your financial habits and increase your savings.	• Grow your emergency fund • Increase your income • Invest consistently • Start building long-term goals (e.g. home, travel, business) • Improve your financial knowledge	You build momentum and your money starts working for you.
YEARS 4-6	**BUILD WEALTH** Make smart financial moves that grow your wealth.	• Invest more and diversify • Consider property or other wealth-building assets • Review and optimise your tax strategy • Increase passive income streams • Protect your income and assets (insurance, estate plan)	Your wealth grows faster and you build financial security.
YEARS 7-10	**BUILD FREEDOM** Prepare for financial independence and live life on your terms.	• Continue investing for long-term growth • Grow and protect your assets • Plan for retirement • Review your goals and adjust • Give back and create a legacy	You enjoy more freedom, choices, and peace of mind for the future.

THE ROADMAP TO REMEMBER

- Start where you are.
- Use what you have.
- Do what you can.
- Stay consistent.
- Trust the process.

THE BIG PICTURE

Wealth isn't built overnight.
It's built one decision at a time.
Ten years from now, you'll thank yourself for starting today.

REMEMBER: Your future is created by what you do today, not tomorrow.
Small steps every day lead to big results over time.

Glossary

Asset

Something you own that has value or has the potential to increase in value or generate income, such as property, shares, or a business.

Bond

A type of investment where you lend money to a government or company in exchange for regular interest payments and the return of your original investment at the end of an agreed period.

Capital Growth

An increase in the value of an investment over time.

Compound Interest

Interest earned on both your original money and the interest it has already earned. Over time, this can significantly increase the growth of your savings or investments.

Debt

Money borrowed that must be repaid, usually with interest.

Diversification

Spreading your investments across different types of assets to help reduce risk.

Dividend

A payment some companies make to shareholders from their profits.

Emergency Fund

Money set aside to cover unexpected expenses such as medical bills, job loss, or urgent repairs.

Equity

The difference between the value of your property and the amount you still owe on your home loan.

ETF (Exchange-Traded Fund)

A fund that holds a collection of investments, such as shares or bonds, allowing you to invest in many assets through a single investment.

Expenses

The money you spend on goods and services.

Financial Freedom

Having enough income or savings to make life choices without being completely dependent on a regular pay cheque.

Inflation

The gradual increase in the price of goods and services over time, reducing the purchasing power of money.

Interest

Money paid for borrowing money or earned from saving or investing money.

Investment

Something purchased with the expectation that it will grow in value or generate income in the future.

Lifestyle Inflation

The tendency to increase your spending as your income increases, making it more difficult to build wealth.

Mortgage

A loan used to purchase property, usually repaid over many years.

Passive Income

Income that continues to be earned after the initial work or investment has been made, often requiring less ongoing effort than active employment.

Portfolio

The collection of investments owned by an individual.

Principal

The original amount of money invested or borrowed, before interest or investment returns.

Return on Investment (ROI)

The profit or loss made on an investment, usually expressed as a percentage of the amount invested.

Risk

The possibility that an investment may lose value or not perform as expected.

Shares

Small ownership interests in a company. People who own shares are known as shareholders.

Superannuation

The Australian retirement savings system, where employers generally contribute money towards an employee's retirement. Other countries have similar retirement savings schemes under different names.

Tax Deduction

An eligible expense that may reduce the amount of income on which you pay tax, depending on the tax laws in your country.

Wealth

The total value of everything you own, less everything you owe.

Yield

The income generated by an investment, often expressed as a percentage of its value. Examples include dividends from shares or rent from an investment property.

WORKSHEET 1

Net Worth Snapshot

SEE WHERE YOU STAND. PLAN WHERE YOU'RE GOING.

Your net worth is simply what you own (assets) minus what you owe (liabilities). It gives you a clear picture of your financial position today.

ASSETS

Everything you own that has value.

ASSET CATEGORY	ESTIMATED VALUE (AUD)
Home (Market Value)	$ ________
Savings Accounts	$ ________
Investments (Shares, ETFs, managed funds)	$ ________
Superannuation	$ ________
Vehicles	$ ________
Personal Assets (Jewellery, electronics, furniture, etc.)	$ ________
Other Assets (Business, collectibles, other)	$ ________
TOTAL ASSETS	$ ________

LIABILITIES

Everything you owe or are responsible for.

LIABILITY CATEGORY	OUTSTANDING AMOUNT (AUD)
Mortgage / Home Loan	$ ________
Credit Cards	$ ________
Car Loan	$ ________
Personal Loans	$ ________
Student Loans	$ ________
Other Loans (HECS/HELP, business loan, etc.)	$ ________
Other Liabilities (Pay later services, tax debt, etc.)	$ ________
TOTAL LIABILITIES	$ ________

YOUR NET WORTH
Total Assets minus Total Liabilities

$ ________________

UNDERSTAND YOUR NUMBER.

- A positive net worth means your assets are greater than your liabilities.
- A negative net worth means you owe more than you own.
- The goal is to grow your assets, reduce your liabilities, and increase your net worth over time.

Review your net worth every 6–12 months.

WORKSHEET 2

Monthly Money Check

TRACK IT. UNDERSTAND IT. IMPROVE IT.

This simple check-in helps you see where your money comes from, **where it goes**, and how you're building your future.

MONTH: ____________________

1. INCOME – WHAT CAME IN

SOURCE OF INCOME	AMOUNT (AUD)
Salary / Wage	$
Business Income	$
Investments / Dividends	$
Rental Income	$
Side Hustle / Freelance	$
Other Income	$
TOTAL INCOME	**$**

2. EXPENSES – WHAT WENT OUT

EXPENSE CATEGORY	AMOUNT (AUD)
Housing (Rent / Mortgage)	$
Utilities (Electricity, Water, Gas, Internet)	$
Groceries / Household	$
Transport (Fuel, Public Transport, Car)	$
Insurance (Health, Car, Home, Life)	$
Debt Repayments	$
Personal (Health, Clothing, Hair, etc.)	$
Entertainment / Dining Out	$
Other Expenses	$
TOTAL EXPENSES	**$**

3. SAVINGS & INVESTING

CATEGORY	AMOUNT (AUD)
Emergency Fund	$
Savings Goals	$
Investments (Shares, ETFs, Funds, etc.)	$
Superannuation (Additional)	$
Other	$
TOTAL SAVINGS & INVESTING	**$**

4. MONTHLY SUMMARY

Total Income		$ ________
Total Expenses	–	$ ________
Total Savings & Investing	–	$ ________
MONEY LEFT OVER	=	$

A positive number means you're on track!
A negative number means it's time to adjust your spending.

5. NOTES

____

____

____

____

____

6. REFLECTION

What went well this month?

____

What could I improve next month?

____

One financial goal I'm working on:

____

CONSISTENCY CREATES CLARITY.
Check in every month. Small changes today lead to big results tomorrow.

Small steps.
Big future.

WORKSHEET 3

Ten-Year Wealth Plan

A VISION WITHOUT A PLAN IS JUST A WISH.

Use this worksheet to clarify your financial goals, map out your actions, and stay focused on what matters most.

TODAY'S DATE: ____ / ____ / ________ STARTING NET WORTH: $ __________

	1. CURRENT POSITION	2. GOALS (10 YEARS)	3. ACTION PLAN
	Where are you financially today? Be honest and specific.	Where do you want to be in 10 years?	What steps will get you there? List the key actions you will take.
INCOME Total monthly income	$ ________ Source(s): ________	$ ________ Source(s): ________	• ________ • ________ • ________
SAVINGS Emergency fund + Cash savings	$ ________ Months of expenses: ____	$ ________ Months of expenses: ____	• ________ • ________ • ________
INVESTMENTS Investments (shares, ETFs, funds, etc.)	$ ________ Asset mix: ________	$ ________ Target asset mix: ________	• ________ • ________ • ________
PROPERTY Details / Investment properties	$ ________ Details: ________	$ ________ Details: ________	• ________ • ________ • ________
DEBT Outstanding debts & loans	$ ________ Details: ________	$ ________ Goal: ________	• ________ • ________ • ________
LIFESTYLE What matters most to you?	________	________	• ________ • ________ • ________

4. REVIEW & TRACK YOUR PROGRESS

Review your plan regularly and update as needed.	REVIEW DATE: ___ / ___ / ___ NOTES: ________	REVIEW DATE: ___ / ___ / ___ NOTES: ________	REVIEW DATE: ___ / ___ / ___ NOTES: ________	REVIEW DATE: ___ / ___ / ___ NOTES: ________

THE FUTURE YOU WANT STARTS WITH THE PLAN YOU MAKE TODAY.
Stay consistent. Be patient. Your future self will thank you.

Plan today.
Take action.
Build your future.

WORKSHEET 4

Investment Diversification Checklist

DON'T PUT ALL YOUR EGGS IN ONE BASKET.

Diversifying your investments helps spread risk and increases the potential for more stable, long-term returns. Use this checklist to build a balanced portfolio that works for you.

DATE: ____ / ____ / ____   CURRENT INVESTMENT EXPERIENCE: ☐ Beginner ☐ Some Experience ☐ Experienced

ASSET CLASS	DESCRIPTION	BENEFITS	INCLUDED IN MY PORTFOLIO?			TARGET ALLOCATION (%)
			YES	NO	PLANNING TO	
CASH & CASH EQUIVALENTS	Savings accounts, term deposits, money market funds.	• High liquidity • Low risk • Capital preservation	☐	☐	☐	______ %
SHARES / EQUITIES	Individual shares or index funds listed on stock exchanges.	• Long-term growth • Potential for higher returns • Ownership in businesses	☐	☐	☐	______ %
EXCHANGE TRADED FUNDS (ETFs)	Funds that track an index, sector, or asset class and trade on exchanges.	• Diversified exposure • Lower costs • Easy to buy and sell	☐	☐	☐	______ %
PROPERTY / REAL ESTATE	Residential, commercial, REITs (real estate investment trusts).	• Income potential • Capital growth • Inflation hedge	☐	☐	☐	______ %
FIXED INCOME / BONDS	Government or corporate bonds, term deposits, bond funds.	• Regular income • Lower volatility • Diversifies portfolio	☐	☐	☐	______ %
INTERNATIONAL INVESTMENTS	Overseas shares, ETFs, or international funds.	• Global diversification • Exposure to other economies • Reduces country risk	☐	☐	☐	______ %
ALTERNATIOVE INVESTMENTS	Commodities, gold, hedge funds, private equity, collectibles.	• Low correlation to markets • Potential for high returns • Adds diversification	☐	☐	☐	______ %
OTHER	Any other investments you are considering.	• Custom to your goals • Adds unique opportunities	☐	☐	☐	______ %
				TOTAL TARGET ALLOCATION		100%

NOTES & THOUGHTS

____

____

____

____

PORTFOLIO DIVERSIFICATION CHECK

A well-diversified portfolio should:

- ☐ Include a mix of different asset classes
- ☐ Match your risk tolerance and time horizon
- ☐ Balance growth potential with stability
- ☐ Not be overly concentrated in one area or asset

Review your portfolio at least once a year or when your goals or life circumstances change.

DIVERSIFY TODAY. PROTECT TOMORROW. GROW OVER TIME.

Diversification doesn't guarantee profits or protect against losses, but it can help you ride out the ups and downs on your way to your goals.

Stay diversified.
Stay focused.
Stay on track.

WORKSHEET 5

Financial Goals

A GOAL WITHOUT A PLAN IS JUST A WISH.

Write down your financial goals, why they matter to you, and the steps you will take to achieve them.

DATE: ____ / ____ / ______

YOUR WHY: What does financial freedom mean to you?

____

1. SHORT-TERM GOALS (1 YEAR)

Goals you want to achieve within the next 12 months.

MY GOALS:

1. ______________
2. ______________
3. ______________

WHY IT MATTERS:

____

ESTIMATED COST:

$ ______________

$ ______________

$ ______________

ACTION STEPS:

What steps will you take?

☐ ______________

☐ ______________

☐ ______________

TARGET DATE: ___ / ___ / _____

2. MID-TERM GOALS (1 – 5 YEARS)

Goals you want to achieve within the next 1 to 5 years.

MY GOALS:

1. ______________
2. ______________
3. ______________

WHY IT MATTERS:

____

ESTIMATED COST:

$ ______________

$ ______________

$ ______________

ACTION STEPS:

What steps will you take?

☐ ______________

☐ ______________

☐ ______________

TARGET DATE RANGE:

From: ____ / ____ / _____

To: ____ / ____ / _____

3. LONG-TERM GOALS (5+ YEARS)

Goals you want to achieve in more than 5 years.

MY GOALS:

1. ______________
2. ______________
3. ______________

WHY IT MATTERS:

____

ESTIMATED COST:

$ ______________

$ ______________

$ ______________

ACTION STEPS:

What steps will you take?

☐ ______________

☐ ______________

☐ ______________

TARGET DATE RANGE:

From: ____ / ____ / _____

To: ____ / ____ / _____

PROGRESS TRACKER

Review your goals regularly and track your progress.

GOAL REVIEW	REVIEW DATE	PROGRESS (What have you achieved?)	WHAT'S WORKING WELL?	WHAT CAN I IMPROVE?
Short-Term Goals	___ / ___ / _____			
Mid-Term Goals	___ / ___ / _____			
Long-Term Goals	___ / ___ / _____			

REMEMBER:

- Break big goals into small steps.
- Be consistent and stay patient.
- Review, adjust, and keep moving forward.

YOU CAN DO THIS!

Small steps today create a better tomorrow. ♥

Continue the Journey with A.M. Hartley

If this book resonated with you, you may also enjoy these other titles exploring relationships, identity, resilience, personal growth, and the human experience.

Relationships & Emotional Wellbeing

The Axe Forgets, the Tree Remembers: Living with Emotional Cruelty and the Quiet Work of Reclaiming Yourself

Between Love and Hate: How Intimacy Turns Into Punishment—and What a Fair Ending Could Look Like

When Kindness Costs You: Boundaries, Self-Worth, and the Hidden Cost of Pleasing Others

Living Without Permission: Power, Memory, and the Right to Self-Determination

Quiet Love: What Lasting Relationships Really Look Like

It Was Just a Bet: Why We Marry, Why We Cheat, and Why Some Stay

Ending Sacrifice Without Safeguards: A Guide for Women to Value Themselves and Prepare for the Future

The High-Functioning Woman's Guide to Boundaries: How to Stop Over-Giving, Reduce Resentment, and Reclaim Your Time

If It Brings You Peace and Strength: Why Self-Care Is Essential—and What It Really Means

Understanding the Narcissist: The Mind Behind the Mask.

The Quiet Weight of Loneliness: Understanding Why We Feel More Disconnected Than Ever

Personal Growth & Self-Reflection

Grow Through Flow: Poems About Change, Renewal, and Becoming

Bridges: Poems to Help You Move Forward with Confidence

In This Season: Grow: How Small, Intentional Steps Create Lasting Success

Self-Doubt: The Quiet Price of Hesitation

When Time Steps Onto the Stage: Reflections on Time, Ageing, and Participation in Life

Secret Person of the Heart: What Our Alter Egos Reveal About Who We Truly Are

The Black Cockatoo: On Trauma, Meaning, and the Quiet Work of Healing

Identity, Society & Culture

Disconnected: Migration, Identity, and the Quiet Complexity of Starting Again

The In-Between Generation: Identity, Systems, and the Children of Migration

For Our Menfolk: Reflections on Boys and Masculinity in a Time of Cultural Transition

Paths We Have Walked: A Reflection on History, Place, and the Traces We Leave Behind

Finding Genuine Meaning in the Age of AI: Technology, Vulnerability, and the Quiet Work of Staying Human

Collateral Damage: The Language of Acceptable Loss in War and Security

A Mother's Pain: Addiction, Loss, and the Hidden Pressures Facing Families Worldwide

Thank You

Thank you for reading *The Quiet Weight of Loneliness: Understanding Why We Feel More Disconnected Than Ever*.

I hope these pages have helped you better understand loneliness—not only as a personal experience, but as something shaped by the changing world around us.

If this book has given you a new perspective, offered reassurance, or reminded you that the need for connection is one of the most human experiences we share, then I am truly grateful that it found its way to you.

If you have a moment, I would greatly appreciate it if you could leave a review where you purchased this book.

Reviews help other readers discover books like this. They also let people who may be feeling isolated or disconnected know that they are not alone in what they are experiencing.

Whether your review is a few sentences or simply a star rating, your support means more than you know.

Connect with A.M. Hartley

If you'd like to hear about future books and reflections from A.M. Hartley, I'd love to stay in touch.

Books:
https://books2read.com/ap/RQJrK6/AM-Hartley

Email:
amhartleywrites@gmail.com

Facebook:
https://www.facebook.com/a.m.hartleywrites

Instagram:
https://www.instagram.com/a.m.hartley

TikTok:
www.tiktok.com@a.m.hartley

Thank you once again for allowing me to be part of your journey.

– **A.M. Hartley**

www.ingramcontent.com/pod-product-compliance
Lightning Source LLC
LaVergne TN
LVHW050822061126
851857LV00012B/930